Do
Greater
Things

Do
Greater
Things

Following in Jesus' Footsteps

Felicia Blanco Searcy

Unity Village, MO 64065-0001

Do Greater Things

First edition 2009; fifth printing 2011

Unity Books are available at special discounts for bulk purchases for study groups, book clubs, sales promotions, book signings or fundraising. To place an order, call the Unity Customer Care Department at 1-866-236-3571 or email *wholesaleaccts@unityonline.org*.

Bible quotations are from the New Revised Standard Version unless otherwise noted.

Cover design by: Jenny Hahn
Interior design by: The Covington Group

Library of Congress Control Number: 2009938367
ISBN 978-0-87159-341-2
CanadaBN 13252 0933 RT

Contents

Dedication

I dedicate this book to my husband, Michael, for his unending support and love, and to my mother, who never wavered in her faith in me and my abilities. I also give thanks to all of those spiritual revolutionaries who went before me, paving the way to my own spiritual growth and evolution.

Introduction

In John 14:12 Jesus said, "Very truly, I tell you, the one who believes in me will also do the works that I do and, in fact, will do greater works than these, because I am going to the Father." In this summons, Jesus said that we have the potential to repeat what he did, and he went on to tell us that our abilities do not stop there, but that we are meant to do more.

His bold declaration claims that there is more work to be done in our world and, furthermore, it is to be done by each of us. His words invite us into a new way of being with ourselves, one another and, ultimately, God. As we redefine these relationships by living his words and actions, we see how we can evolve as spiritual beings. As we grow, we also see how, like Jesus, we can impact and serve our world.

The above quote from Jesus has worked its way into my consciousness and challenges my very existence on a daily basis. I ask myself regularly, *Do I believe in Jesus, and if so, what do I believe about him?* Then comes the big question: *If I believe in Jesus, why am I not repeating and surpassing what he did? Why am I not following this very simple direction?*

We have made progress over the past two millennia toward Jesus' vision of a more compassionate, generous, inclusive and connected world. We are more aware of one another's suffering and more willing to step in during personal and global tragedies. We have created social welfare programs to help individuals in need, and people from around the world rushed to help in the wake of Hurricane Katrina and the Indian Ocean tsunami. As a global society, we are also more aware of the issues stemming from poverty, hunger, human rights violations and the abuse of our planet.

This is all a testament to our increased sensitivity to the suffering of others and a greater awareness of how we are all connected. Yet it is clear that we still fall short of the example that Jesus gave us. We still battle with one another on a personal and a global scale. We hurl insults at one another and allow our prejudices to dictate our actions and laws.

Jesus' words challenge us to look at our lives in light of his and to examine our disconnection from one another. His life also demands that before we can carry out his teachings, we must look at the mythology we have created around Jesus that binds us rather than frees us. If we study his teachings from a different perspective, we can redefine the essence of his message and his life. We can then begin to see ways to use our own lives to carry on who he was and what he taught.

In these pages I explore the meaning and practicality of Jesus' statement. He saw our potential and our spiritual magnificence. He saw what was possible for each of us, and he longed for us to experience that possibility too. He also saw that the well-being of our brothers and sisters depends on each of us discovering our spiritual glory.

Introduction

As we evolve, we will realize this truth: that we can follow in Jesus' footsteps. And once we develop our ability to repeat what he did, we will be able to focus on our ultimate goal, which is to go beyond his example. But we must learn to walk before we can run. The purpose of this book is to help us grow into the example that Jesus gave us so that we can, yes, even surpass him. Join me on the journey.

I also reveal my own story as well as those of others who have shared their experiences with me over the years. Mine has been a journey of rediscovery and growth, along with a process of releasing and shedding old paradigms and superstitions that kept me from believing that I could repeat what Jesus did. I had a deep ache to know God in the same intimate way that Jesus knew God. This meant trading in my tired version of myself as a worthless sinner for the image that Jesus had of me: an incredible, irreplaceable creation of God.

As I embarked on this journey, I was supported by others who have asked the same questions and entered the same unknown places that I found myself in. They freely shared their wisdom, knowledge and experiences with me. They gave me support in person, on the phone or in the pages of their books. I know many of them intimately, while others I would not recognize if I met them on the street. The lessons I have learned are relevant to everyone: We all long for the same things, and we can support one another by sharing our experiences, strength and wisdom. This fosters our collective evolution toward the vision that Jesus had for us.

As a minister, I have also been privileged to continue Jesus' legacy by assisting other people along their spiritual path and witnessing and supporting their spiritual maturation. Like me, many of them were disenchanted with what they had been taught about Jesus. So often they could not reconcile what they had heard with what resonated in their hearts.

Just as others who went before me gave me permission to question and change my understanding of Jesus, I give people in my congregation the space to suspend what they have heard in the past so that they can have a different experience of our master teacher. I invite them to see God big enough to handle their questions so that they can discover a Jesus who supports them spiritually. This is what I hope to create for you, the reader, as well.

This change in our perception of Jesus is a result of deliberate practice. The challenge is to take what we learn and apply the ideas to the smallest details of our lives. I personally needed a way to take the principles I was discovering in the pages of a book or from the mouth of a teacher and apply them to the grittiest moments of my life. They had to have practical meaning for me. I also needed things simple. In order to feel that I was making some kind of progress toward Jesus' edict, I needed a structured plan that gave me something tangible to do.

When I examined Jesus' life, I saw patterns of behavior that enabled him to do what he did. I then identified nine practices in his life that continue to create radical changes in

Introduction

the way I live my own life as I adopt them as my own. They are:

- Vision
- Faith
- Prayer
- Humility
- Forgiveness
- Gratitude
- Community
- Death
- Service

Any one of these practices is powerful in and of itself. Taken together, they can change not only your own life but the world.

In this book, I address each spiritual practice in a separate chapter. At the end of each chapter, I include specific activities associated with that practice that you can begin to do immediately. These activities are meant to make the spiritual disciplines come alive for you. They encourage you to go beyond abstract ideas to concrete action. Faith without works is dead. It is changed perspective coupled with action that will bring about Jesus' vision of heaven here on earth.

Chapter 1, which precedes the discussion of the spiritual practices, looks at the beliefs we hold about Jesus and why they are important. They frame our relationship with him, so it is vital that our encounter with our Way Shower supports our endeavor to repeat what he did and then surpass it.

I am not a Bible scholar. I sit in awe when I read biblical experts like Marcus Borg and Bishop John Shelby Spong. Their words, along with those of many others, have opened a door for me to think differently about Jesus and God. As I read how others have asked the same questions and drink in their knowledge and information, I rejoice that there is a different way from the one I was taught. I see that there is a way that leads me to the experience of wholeness, life and joy—all the things that Jesus promised us. I am more alive as a result of having found an alternative to my traditional upbringing, and I experience moments of deep mystical union that allow me to offer more compassion to, and appreciation for, the people in my life.

That is my hope for you as well. My desire is that you will be able to suspend judgment and fear in order to explore a different vision of Jesus. That means we have to question our assumptions about God as well. Make God big enough to question and call on the carpet regarding the inconsistencies in what we are taught. Trust me when I say that God will not retaliate. Give yourself permission to have a nontraditional experience of God. If you are not changed in some way, you are free to return to your old paradigms and pretend you never picked up this book.

A Note About the Pronouns I Use for God

I do want to say a word about the way I refer to God. God is usually referred to as "he," and as a result, for a long time I felt alienated. As a woman, I often found it difficult to feel included in the conversation. Referring to God this way also limits God; it creates the illusion that God is a being outside ourselves—loving, but separate nevertheless.

One of the primary functions of this book is to challenge our paradigms and fundamental picture of God. I do this by referring to God differently than ever before. I mix pronouns, using the male and female gender terms as well as the impersonal pronoun "it." This reflects Jesus' experience with God as both immanent and transcendent. If my use of any one of these terms causes you discomfort, I invite you to look at the source of your discomfort and allow it to reflect for you your current beliefs about God. It is an invitation to expand your image and experience of God.

My intention with this book is to invite all of us to move into a deeper, more mystical experience with Jesus and God. As we begin to do so, we collectively unleash the power of Spirit that is within each of us. In turn, we use this inherent power to do our part to bring alive, here and now, the vision of the kingdom of God that Jesus painted for us so beautifully! Join me in the discovery of a new Jesus so that we can learn how to do greater things!

Together in the Christ,

Rev. Felicia Searcy

Do Greater Things

∞

∞

-1-

Believe in Me

What does it mean to believe in someone? *Merriam-Webster's Collegiate Dictionary* defines *believe* as "to accept as true, genuine or real; to have a firm conviction as to the goodness, efficacy, or ability of something." Jesus told us in John 14:12, "Very truly, I tell you, the one who believes in me will also do the works that I do and, in fact, will do greater works than these, because I am going to the Father." We can do what he did when we believe in him!

Think for a moment: Whom or what do you believe in? Who in your life is true and real? And how did you develop these opinions? The people you believe in have earned your respect because of their ability or knowledge. You trust what they say or do because you have seen that their actions match their words. As a result, you are willing to follow where they lead. Because of their inspiration and example, you also see how you have something to offer. You feel their support as you begin to take on new ventures.

Life Journeys

My mother is an ongoing source of inspiration for me. I believe her when she says that it is possible to achieve our dreams, because she has done so in the face of seemingly insurmountable odds. My mom struggled with addiction and depression for most of her life, yet she had a dream to be an artist. More important, she wanted a place that she could call her studio. With lots of hard work, patience and ingenuity, she was able to accomplish both goals.

She owns an old farmhouse in northern Wisconsin that has an old, dilapidated chicken coop on the property. When she first saw the chicken house, the walls were falling down, the roof was caved in and there were years of chicken poop piled on the floor. But she saw the potential.

For four to five years, she worked on bringing it back to life. When I called her during that time, she would excitedly share her progress. Oftentimes it was as simple as having cleared out a certain amount of the floor. Eventually other people became believers and went over to help her. Over time the floor was cleaned, the walls were restored and the roof was replaced.

Now when I go to visit, we take our coffee and dessert and head out to her studio to admire her latest piece of artwork. I believe her when she tells me that I, too, can achieve my heart's desire.

My mother's influence extends through me to those I touch. As I share what I have gained from her, her words come out of my mouth, and my actions reflect her presence in my life.

Today I believe in Jesus because he practiced what he taught, changing the very fabric of our world. He continues to live on through each of us. He gave us an unbeatable model that, when followed, will lead us to a life that transcends anything we have ever imagined or experienced. When we read what he had to say and about the acts he performed, we sense his authenticity and power. We see how he has dramatically affected people from 2,000 years ago to today.

Yet I have not always felt this way about Jesus. In fact, for many years I was afraid of him and the idea of following him. People told me that in order to follow the master, I had to be willing to suffer and sacrifice as he did. Others said that I was a lowly sinner, and, therefore, Jesus had had to endure a horrible death to save me. My exposures to him left me feeling despondent, unworthy and incapable of much of anything. I felt defeated before I even got started.

My college roommate and I talked incessantly about what God expected from us. His standards were too high, I felt, and I would never measure up because of an imagined black spot on my soul that was impossible to remove, no matter what I did. Religion taught me about Jesus' sacrifice and implied that God expected nothing less from us. My conversations with clergy, in which I asked how I could return to God's good graces, left me feeling even more alienated. No matter what I did, it would not be enough. Yet questioning any of these feelings was a breach of faith. To question was to risk angering God and facing abandonment.

But not to question was to die. I was desperate. I longed to know God, to feel a deep connection. My life consisted of trying to earn God's love, and yet I always felt that I was missing the mark. I had resigned myself to a life of loneliness, rejection and isolation. I felt as though I didn't have a right to be alive anyway, so what harm could I do by questioning God? If God was really that unapproachable and judgmental, I had nothing to lose, and I had nowhere else to go. With my soul on the line, I had to take my chances.

Deep down, I knew that this was not the kind of experience that Jesus wanted us to have with God. It was time to go with my inner stirrings to explore another view of God and Jesus. In beginning my search, I started reading extensively, as well as listening to people who had other perspectives. I discovered a whole population of people out there whose point of view was very different from anything I had been exposed to before, and I eagerly soaked up their ideas and experiences.

It was scary at first. I had to keep giving myself permission to question what I had been taught. I discovered that God did not expect me to accept everything on blind faith; rather, she had gifted me with an intellect to use in order to question and learn. So despite my doubts, I kept listening. I felt pulled along a new path and, once on it, was not willing to revert to the old image of a punishing, distant God.

I began to see myself differently. For the first time in my life, I saw my own divine nature and potential. New worlds opened up for me. I started to have both wonderful and scary thoughts and feelings that I did not understand and could not explain.

The truth of original goodness replaced the theory of original sin. The image of God as judger and withholder melted away, replaced by an experience of beauty and compassion. Everything in view became sacred, as I no longer saw God as something separate. A different experience of God began to emerge from the depths of my being—one of love, life and transformation—along with a sense of deep connection to the Creator. I began to get an inkling of what Jesus meant by his teachings and life.

I realized that the way I perceived Jesus had changed. Jesus is with me throughout my day, blanketing me in his love and strength. He is my guide and example. He meant for us to look to him as a guide or counselor, as an older brother showing the way. Digging deeper and contemplating his words further, I discovered that he meant for us to lean on him as we travel our own path of awakening.

What Did Jesus Do?

Jesus knows things about me that I can only imagine. He extends his hand and invites me to follow him to new heights.

He continues to be a constant presence, encouraging me to transcend my tired, broken perception of myself in order to experience and broaden the reality of God in my own life.

Hermit, priest, retreat leader and writer Cynthia Bourgeault, in her wonderful teaching series *Encountering the Wisdom Jesus*, presented two interpretations of Jesus. The first is *soteriology*—the one most familiar to us in the West—in which Jesus is viewed as a savior. We are taught that we are soiled with original sin and that Jesus came to sacrifice himself in order for us to find favor with God again. It teaches that Jesus is the only way to salvation.

She also introduced the concept of *sophiology*, which teaches that Jesus came not to save us but to direct our attention back to the reality of who we are as divine expressions of God. It views Jesus as our compass and way-shower, directing us toward a different experience of God. Jesus wanted to show us what was in store for us if we followed his path.[1]

When you see Jesus as the way-shower, you begin to study him as if you were his apprentice. Like the student of a great master, you copy the nuances of his strokes, hoping to reproduce the same results.

As a result, your excitement builds for Jesus and what he stands for. You begin to identify with him and want to be a part of what he did and taught. Like a container filled to overflowing, you become incapable of keeping your new discovery to yourself. His vision is contagious, and you long for others to experience holiness and goodness. Like Jesus, you begin to see that everyone contains potential for great-ness, and you want to do your part to make that potential real.

As the presence of God grew in Jesus—in other words, as Jesus realized God greater—he recognized how God expressed divine qualities through him into the world. These then became the themes for his life. He became the human embodiment of compassion, generosity, wholeness, abun-dance, life force, justice, inclusiveness, faith and belief in the presence and power of goodness. These qualities are present in everything he did and taught. Once he saw them in him-self, he was able to see them in us and help us see them in ourselves as well.

Introducing us to a whole new experience of God became a key element of Jesus' mission. You cannot follow in his foot-steps if you hold on to the traditional view of God. He intro-duced the world to a God that is no longer something or someone outside of us, waiting to be pleased or displeased. The God that Jesus brings alive is one of love and availa-bility. It is a God that longs for each one of us to experience the richness of life.

These ideas are important because they introduce the hypothesis that we cannot be separated from God's love. It is an ancient struggle. As a species, the more self-conscious we have become, the more isolated and alone we have felt. People felt separated from God 2,000 years ago just as we do today. We can hear the fear and longing in myths and stories across traditions. In many of the tales told in the Bible, God is portrayed as harsh and someone whose wrath is to be avoided.

With the birth of Christianity, writers continued to paint a picture of God as being swift in his punishment of what seemed like minor infractions. God was presented as a supreme being that did things like wipe out entire civilizations with floods because he was displeased with humankind, as well as order his warriors to show no mercy to their enemies.

Jesus knew God differently. He wanted people to know that God's love was available to everyone at all times. The Gospels are filled with images of a loving presence. For example, in the story of the Prodigal Son, Jesus paints a picture of God as a loving father whose only concern was that both of his sons knew of his love for them.

God's Unconditional Love

Let's think about that for a bit. How would your life be different if you really knew that God is always present, all-loving and all-providing? What if you truly knew God as your only reality? Imagine how that would change the way you interacted with the world.

Internally, you would be at peace. You would abandon your need to defend or protect anything because you would understand at a fundamental level that you could lose nothing. You would give up the fight. If you cannot be separated from the presence and mind of God, then it is impossible for you to lose what you really desire.

Knowing God only as love, you could not help sharing this awareness with everyone around you. You would be so filled with the presence of love that you would not be able to contain it—nor would you want to. You would be able to see these same qualities in others too.

It is interesting that Jesus gave only two commandments. In Mark 12:29-31 we read, "'Hear, O Israel: the Lord our God, the Lord is one; you shall love the Lord your God with all your heart, and with all your soul, and with all your mind, and with all your strength.' The second is this, 'You shall love your neighbor as yourself.' There is no other commandment greater than these.'"

According to Matthew 22:40, "On these two commandments hang all the law and the prophets." These two laws brilliantly distill the world's wisdom and laws into two simple statements, and they are all about love. The great thing is that when you experience God as love, you embody love.

In Mark, Jesus was not referring to a warm and fuzzy love; rather, his love is a deep, universal devotion that includes everyone. He was also explaining that when we love God, we love ourselves and our neighbors because we see that we are not separate. As Bourgeault stated, "There is no longer 'us' and 'them.'" We become One. By loving this way, we transform ourselves and those around us.

You can't help being different when you are exposed to this level of unconditional acceptance. The stories and lessons that are told in the Gospels illustrate this. After betraying Jesus three times, Peter went on to establish the Church in Jerusalem because he felt forgiven by Jesus after the resurrection. Mary Magdalene was not only healed from her physical condition of 12 years of hemorrhaging but also went on to become one of Jesus' most powerful supporters and disciples.

Specifically, this kind of love restores people to wholeness. The Bible is filled with stories in which people were healed of whatever ailed them when they went to Jesus. Knowing that we, too, have the power to love and heal, he wants us to unconditionally love ourselves and others into wholeness as well.

Such love also results in abundance. Jesus never went hungry or lacked what he needed. He took care of the physical needs of the people who came to him while he ministered to their spiritual needs. He demonstrated with his teachings and his miracles that God's abundance is everywhere and for everyone.

The Gospels are filled with miracle stories about the healing of sickness, the calming of nature and the feeding of multitudes. The writers give Jesus supernatural powers that result in extraordinary acts of greatness. But the more science reveals about the workings of the Universe, the more unlikely the stories sound.

So is it important to believe that miracles happened as written? Simply put, no. Yet something happened in order for the writer to report an event the way he did. Jesus performed the miracle of seeing his surroundings and people differently. As a result, he was able to tap into the unlimited capacity to express all the qualities of God, a capacity that is present in all of us.

His miracle was one of transformation that happened at a fundamental level. People changed as a result of their association with Jesus, and their lives got better. The onlookers experienced something with him that felt healing and nourishing. When we understand the spirit of the miracle, the magic is no longer necessary because collectively we can then achieve the same results.

We are surrounded by miracles today. The fact that we can pull a cell phone out of our pocket when walking down the street and have a conversation with someone who is hundreds of miles away was inconceivable during Jesus' time. Yet today we see it as mundane, even annoying at times. The miracle is that we discovered the nature of sound and physics that was present all along.

There is the potential for joy, wholeness and expansiveness designed into every moment, and the miracle is when we recognize the constant presence of these qualities all around us. Once we see what is possible, our lives then begin to change. This is what Jesus discovered and invites us to repeat.

Following Jesus means life. A life directed by Spirit or love erases fear and confusion and replaces them with faith and a deep sense of well-being. Following Jesus means becoming more willing to let go of the old to make room for the new. Life is meant to be lived fully, and we trust in the ability and desire of a Creator to fulfill that truth through us. Paradoxically, with Jesus' death, he showed us life.

How Can We Know Heaven?

Fundamentally, Jesus' lessons on love are meant to lead us to the kingdom of God, or kingdom of heaven. This was Jesus' foundational teaching, but just as the message becomes unrecognizable in the telephone game, when the original message gets distorted as it is whispered from one player to the next, what Jesus taught about heaven and the image we have today are completely different. He taught that heaven is an experience that is a result of living as he directed, rather than a place waiting for us upon our death.

Many of us in Western culture have been taught that heaven is a destination that we achieve after living right in this life. Consequently, our attention has been focused on the future rather than the present. Our actions are motivated by a need to bargain for our place in heaven instead of flowing naturally from our God experience. Heaven becomes a place to get to rather than an experience to claim.

Cynthia Bourgeault has suggested that the kingdom of heaven is not a place; instead it is a state of consciousness. It is the mystical experience of union with God. Marcus Borg, in his book *Meeting Jesus Again for the First Time*, described it as "Among you, inside you, and outside you. Neither is it sometime in the future, for it is here, spread out on the earth; people just do not see it."[2]

We are all wired to seek and know God. It is as if we have a God-seeking gene built right into us. Shifting our focus from earning heaven to knowing it in the present moment creates our heaven experience. Jesus found this state of existence, and he wants us to know it as well. His example shows that we can purposely seek union with God, which is the state of heaven.

Once we have achieved this union, it is easy to see how to translate this mystical experience into action. He demonstrated through his own life what happens when deeper union with God becomes our desire. Our capacity for performing unprecedented acts of compassion and generosity expands in indescribable ways. We see things differently, and therefore we live differently. We begin to automatically replicate what Jesus did.

Each of you will demonstrate this level of love or state of heaven in your own unique way as you challenge the things that keep you separated from God and others. Learning to love this way, you strip naked your judgments, fears and prejudices. As a result, all that is left is God. When you live from a place of no separation between yourself, God and others, you bring alive the potential for true greatness that is embedded in each moment. And that is heaven!

The single quality that enabled Jesus to love and perform the way he did was his knowledge that he was one with the "Father." It all boils down to this single truth, which is what he challenges you to repeat: He longs for you to know union with God as he did. He knows that when you follow his lead by knowing yourself fused with God, the rest will take care of itself. You will naturally perform the acts of greatness that he did, and with the same wisdom and faith.

As we realize our union with Spirit, we give hope to those who witness our transformation. For the first time, people who took seriously what Jesus said had hope that there was something more to their lives than the way they were living. He was able to convince people that they had value. When they were in his presence, they knew that they were precious in God's eyes. We are offered the same hope when we seek union with God.

It is important to note at this juncture that Jesus did not do anything for personal gain. Everything he did was to serve the glory of God, which translates into serving humanity. Jesus faced his own fears and temptations and came out of the "battle in the desert" clear and centered in his purpose. He emerged with the understanding that his life was no longer his own; rather, he was God's instrument of transformation. Because Jesus was able to let go of the need for personal gain and credit, he became the empty vessel through which God was able to express itself.

This is our challenge. In order to follow Jesus, we, too, must be willing to set aside our personal agendas and need for recognition. We must face our fears and temptations so that we can gain clarity about our purpose. As we commit to our spiritual path, we will regard ourselves as God's instrument.

See Yourself in Jesus

One of the biggest obstacles facing us as we undertake this call to repeat what Jesus did is the salvation myth. Because of the prevailing belief that humankind needs to be saved in order to be worthy in the sight of God, we are unable to identify with Jesus. In order to repeat what someone else has done, we must be able to see ourselves in that person, even if it is only in the form of potential.

Instead of following the path that Jesus laid out for us, we have made him our object of worship. We put distance between him and his acts in a way that makes Jesus unique. It seems to be easier to see Jesus as one-of-a-kind because it gets us off the hook of having to do the hard work that is necessary to replicate and surpass what he did. This is exactly what Jesus did not want to happen. He urged us not to make him the object of our adoration. He continually directed us back to the Father within as the source of our power.

Our potential gets covered up by our sense of unworthiness. Religions both past and present have taken Jesus' message and distorted it in a way that renders people helpless. We don't see ourselves the way he did and does: glorious and full of potential. We find it incredibly difficult to believe that Jesus wanted to unleash our splendor. We have been programmed to think of ourselves as sinners and worthless, to the point where we need a Messiah to come and rescue us.

The crucial point about a Messiah mentality is that in order for us to be saved, there is something we need to be saved from. Traditional teachings say that God sent his only son to save us from our sins because ultimately God was going to judge us as unacceptable. So the message was that while Jesus came to save us from our sins, in reality he came to save us from God's wrath.

This message encourages feelings of fear and unworthiness. It is debilitating at its core. We are told that there is hope in this message, but the reason for the message in the first place negates any hope we may experience as a result of it. It is certainly not a message that suggests we can repeat what Jesus did. In fact, it tells us that not only are we not capable of repeating it, but there is something inherently wrong in entertaining the thought.

We must be willing to rewrite this script if we are going to follow Jesus in his path. It doesn't make sense to embrace the idea that we can accomplish what he called us to do while perpetuating the myth that we are worthless and need saving.

Any good teacher knows that the sign of a great lesson is when the student is able to take what the instructor has given and use it to surpass the teacher. It is a small, insecure teacher who wants to keep the student dependent on him or her. It is a shallow, fearful teacher who needs to be smarter than his or her student. A humble teacher will celebrate when a student takes what is offered and goes on to use it to make a greater contribution.

Jesus was a great teacher. It is difficult to imagine that he was so ego-driven that he would not want us to repeat what he did. Everything he did was in service to God. There can be no greater service to God and humanity than to enlist and equip others to continue the work one has started. Jesus needs us to transcend our perceived human limitations so that we can evolve into the spiritual beings we were created to be in order to carry on his work.

We have reason to feel confident in our own potential ability to do what our teacher did—it's not just a matter of faith. The Gospels report that the disciples were able to repeat many of Jesus' actions after his resurrection, which we will address later. For now we are functioning under the assumption that Jesus' followers had a mystical encounter with the risen Christ that resulted in a monumental breakthrough for them.

It was reported that they had the power to heal and raise people from the dead. They freed themselves from prisons and influenced people by the thousands. They created communities where resources were shared and hierarchies were no longer the focus. They began to create the kind of world that Jesus had dreamed of, showing that it is possible for us to perform extraordinary acts as well. We, too, have the power to free ourselves from the prison of self-imposed limitations and restore ourselves and others to wholeness.

Nature's Infinite Possibilities

Everything in nature is repeatable. When someone breaks a perceived barrier or challenges current understanding of a natural law, it paves the way for the same action to be repeated. There are no exceptions in nature. Jesus gave us the initial example, and the first-century disciples showed that it was possible to replicate what he did. They believed in Jesus, his teachings and his actions. They performed the miracles in his name and nature. Their actions reinforce that possibility for us.

Jesus did not have magical powers, and he didn't do what he did because he was God's favorite son. He simply had a greater understanding of the nature of God, which allowed him to apply natural and spiritual laws better. When we break through limiting paradigms, we, too, can apply the laws to our lives in greater measure.

Flight is a great example of this. For centuries, people believed that flight was impossible. The common belief was that if God wanted humankind to fly, "he" would have given humankind wings. Then along came visionaries who knew that somehow humankind was meant to conquer the skies. These courageous pioneers added to the puzzle of flight with each new discovery.

The Wright brothers brought it all together with their famous flight at Kitty Hawk. They broke the barrier of the day that said flight was impossible. For most of us today, our greatest concern when flying is whether or not there will be a screaming child behind us. We watch the space shuttle take off and land with very little attention or fanfare. Flight has become commonplace.

The laws of flight have been present since the beginning of time. No one invented them. Instead, inventors discovered them and put them to practical use. These forward-thinking individuals defied the common beliefs of their day and followed their instincts, bringing flight from the invisible to the physical.

This same analogy applies to Jesus and to us. All Jesus did was demonstrate the potential that is present at all times. He did not do anything unique or special. Like the possibility of flight, the higher spiritual principles enabling each of us to repeat what Jesus did have always been there, waiting to be discovered, so that we can put them to practical use.

This is why Jesus' words from John 14:12 challenge us to re-evaluate everything we hold sacred. We continue to create paradigms to explain what is possible or not. We have devised our own barriers and justifications for not taking his statement seriously or, on the extreme end, for seeing as a heretic someone who does.

Admittedly, it is mind-boggling, to say the least, to think about what Jesus understood and experienced. It can feel overwhelming to try to measure up to it. So many of us stop before we ever get started because replicating what Jesus did seems like a hopeless cause.

I am frequently reminded how much work I still have to address in my own life in order to accomplish what Jesus commissioned us to do. His lessons on forgiveness remind me of my own tendency to dwell on how others often make me feel like a first-grader. The vitamin supplements lined up in my cabinet to address a number of physical issues remind me how far I have to go to realize his message of wholeness. I catch myself worrying about money or, literally, about what I will wear or eat.

It will take me time to learn these lessons, just as it takes time to learn anything. It may take lifetimes. But why not dedicate myself to Jesus' ideas and plans for me and everyone else? What would I be doing otherwise?

And the wonderful thing is that it is not a black-or-white, linear event. When you commit yourself to the life that Jesus has outlined, you reap the rewards along the way. Life becomes less stressful and scary for you. You feel a deep sense of purpose and direction.

Following this path requires discipline and dedication. It is an attempt to replicate what Jesus did by shifting some very deep beliefs that we have inherited from well-meaning people. It is a glorious journey. It is one filled with hope and purpose and joy, and one that has been paved well for us.

So I invite you to take the journey with me. As you explore each practice, I encourage you to try the suggestions in each chapter. Jesus was a man of action, and his vision requires action on the part of each of us. This book is simply one interpretation of what that action might look like. It is one thing to think something, and quite another to live it. The practices I describe are meant to assist us with living the teachings of Jesus, which will inevitably change the world.

Join me on this path of spiritual revolution and transformation as we begin the journey to repeat and surpass what Jesus dared us to do.

Practicing the Practice

At the end of each chapter, I include specific activities to assist you with developing or deepening your practice. These are not the be-all and end-all; they are simply a way to get you started.

Let's begin by taking stock of where you are. Write down your responses to each of the following:

1. How do you view Jesus? How has your perception of him either enhanced your journey along your spiritual path or distracted you from it? Are you willing to entertain a different perspective of Jesus?

2. Take a moment, close your eyes and ponder Jesus' statement "Very truly, I tell you, the one who believes in me will also do the works that I do and in fact, will do greater works than these, because I am going to the Father." Repeat the statement to yourself. Allow it to roll around in your mind and heart. Feel it on your tongue. What is your visceral reaction? Can you believe in what Jesus tells you? Can you see yourself repeating what he did? If not, can you see yourself having the potential to repeat what he did?

3. Whom or what do you believe in? Who has believed in you, and how have you changed as a result of his or her belief? Whom have you believed in? How has that person affected your life? Can you see his or her influence in your life?

-2-
Vision

Jesus had a vision. It was an idea of what life was supposed to be like, and he wanted to share it with us. He communicated his vision in everything he said and did. Jesus knew that life could be different for his listeners, if only they could change the way they saw the world. He told them, "The kingdom of heaven is at hand" (Matthew 4:17 KJV). In other words, see through my eyes, and see how heaven is here and now.

Vision is a powerful force that takes hold of you and won't let go. It demands that you pay attention and take action once you get a glimpse of it. It is the force that propels you forward and launches you out of your everyday existence. Vision is the dream that replaces the mundane with passion and enthusiasm. With vision, you feel as if you have input into your own life and are no longer haphazardly cast about.

Merriam-Webster's Collegiate Dictionary defines *vision* as "foresight." It is the ability to see beyond the obvious in order to recognize something revolutionary. It is a necessary ingredient of any advancement and invention.

A while back, a small group of committed folks and I pioneered a New Thought church in a small southern town. At the time, people who were looking for an alternative to traditional religion in that community had nowhere to go. Many residents cautioned us not to put our time and energy into this plan, warning that the area was simply too conservative to support a Unity church.

But the vision was not to be ignored or dismissed. It grabbed us with a powerful image of people applying fresh and revolutionary principles in a way that catapulted them into a new spiritual dimension. And the vision did not stop there. It presented a picture of people as catalysts for the awakening of others, creating dramatic change for a better world.

I had no formal training, and none of us knew how to put a church together. I had not even been involved in the business of a church before. Yet we were compelled to follow the voice within that showed an image of what the world could be like. Eight years later, our town has a Unity church where people come together to grow and mature spiritually, and in turn they do their part toward contributing to the evolution of others around them.

A vision expands and serves. It does not contract or detract from anyone else. Vision is principle-motivated and not personality-driven. The dream fosters excitement, originality and creativity. A true vision will bring out the best in people and act as a catalyst for their growth and evolution. The realization of a vision will result in long-lasting, positive effects for everyone.

Vision is enduring and survives its originator. It excites others so that they continue the work necessary to bring it to fruition long after the original founder is gone. Jesus' vision continues to capture our imagination today. Even with the innumerable interpretations throughout history, the flame of his dream remains alive 2,000 years later, waiting for us to pick up the torch to continue his work.

Jesus' vision is applicable to everyone. Great masters of the ages can be heard in his words and teachings. His actions reflect truth, and his invitation leaves no one out. The wonderful thing about his vision is that we can believe in the dream without necessarily having to follow the man. That may sound blasphemous, but a true visionary does not have to be the one from whom others hear the message. He or she simply wants the message heard.

A View of the Kingdom

Jesus referred to his vision as the kingdom of heaven or the kingdom of God. According to one resource, there are 760 references to these terms in the New Testament alone. He told us in Matthew 6:33, "But strive for the kingdom of God and his righteousness, and all these things will be given to you as well." In Mark 1:15 (NIV) he said, "The time has come. The kingdom of God is near."

Jesus' stories depict heaven as a state of wholeness, abundance and inclusion. He compared it to a banquet where everyone is invited but also, in one classic example, to an undesirable mustard seed that contaminates a field. The parable of the mustard seed is often told in order to show the power of faith, but Jesus had a very different idea in mind when he shared it. The account epitomized his image of heaven as a place that left no one out.

Marcus Borg, in *Meeting Jesus Again for the First Time*, explained that farmers did not want mustard growing in their fields. If this renegade plant managed to take hold, it would contaminate the entire field. Farmers worked hard to keep it out so their crops would stay pure. Jesus turned this conventional wisdom on its head when he said that heaven could be compared to a field contaminated with mustard. He challenged what was considered pure and sacred and suggested that heaven occurred when everyone was included. He presented heaven as the state of mind in which there are no barriers between "us and them"; rather, we see ourselves and others as a necessary and holy part of God's design.[1]

There is another beautiful image of heaven in the story of the Prodigal Son. Conventional wisdom sees the story as one of forgiveness and redemption. But there is another meaning when we look deeper. The parable tells of a father with two sons. The younger son had asked for his inheritance so that he could go and squander it in riotous living. He was reduced to the lowest level a Jewish boy could reach when he found himself feeding pigs.

The story then takes a turn. The author tells us that this boy "came to himself" (Luke 15:17). He woke up and realized things would be better for him in his father's house even as a mere servant, so he headed home.

I love this next part of the tale: Before he was even halfway home, his father saw him and rushed toward him, embraced him and welcomed him back. He then put a ring on his son's finger, which, according to Aramaic biblical scholar Rocco Errico, indicates full claim to his identity, and threw one heck of a party. The story never mentions forgiveness. Forgiveness can be inferred. But my heart warms at the fact that the father never said a word about the son's riotous living. He simply opened his arms and welcomed his son back into the fold, no questions asked.

This account conveys a powerful message to us. It tells us that the kingdom of heaven is realized when we know that we are completely accepted for who we are and are entitled to all of God's abundance. This concept replaces the image of God as judger and puts God in the position of nurturer and provider. It suggests that only our thinking can separate us from God's care and abundance. Heaven is available the instant we "come to ourselves."

The story of the Prodigal Son does not end there. Remember the elder brother? He was in a back room somewhere, grumbling about the show for the younger son. He was feeling diminished because he had stayed home, worked hard and followed the rules in hopes that he would receive the same kind of treatment his younger brother was receiving. He refused to join in the festivities, believing that the younger son did not deserve that reception.

In a response that perfectly reflects Jesus' teachings, the father anguished over his elder son's actions, telling him that everything his father possessed had always been available to him. All he needed to do was ask and receive. There was no "earning."

Similarly, heaven patiently waits for us to ready ourselves so that we can receive it. But how do we cultivate the experience of heaven? Through the very goals and ideals that we have for our own lives. Our dreams are God's way of nudging us to expand our capacity to participate in and contribute to life. Our desire for a better life is the catalyst for our growth and evolution. It is the channel through which God shares itself in our world, and becomes the means through which the kingdom of heaven is made manifest on earth.

It is hard for many of us to take our dreams seriously. Somewhere along the line, we may have heard messages telling us, for example, that we could not earn a living doing what we longed to do. Someone may have told us that we were being selfish and should get our head out of the clouds. We may think that our dreams are not realistic. Yet our dreams are the fuel that keeps us moving in the direction of God's plan for us.

Life Journeys

Many courageous souls have shown us what it is to see a vision and follow it in the face of insurmountable odds. There is a woman in our church who has been an inspiration to all of us. She had every reason to give up hope and think that her dreams were never going to come true. She had grown up in the foster care system, married an abusive man, ended up living out of her car after losing everything, and, on top of all of this, had degenerative arthritis.

When I met her she was barely able to walk, lived in public assistance housing and was unable to work. But despite the challenges in her life, she never gave up the dream of walking again and attending college to finish her degree. Her vision blazed like a fire during the darkest times of her life.

She held on to her dream and continued her spiritual practice. She worked with ideas of truth and shifted her perception of herself and others around her. She practiced many of the principles discussed in this book, not because doing so would "make God happy," but because she knew she was entitled to a rich inheritance that she was unable to accept because of her self-image.

After several years of dedicated spiritual practice, she obtained medical insurance that enabled her to have her hips replaced. Once she could walk, she enrolled in the local university and started taking classes. When I saw her most recently, as she was walking into church unassisted, she shared the good news that she had been able to maintain at least a 3.5 grade point average and loved being back in school. She had never let go of the possibility that she could achieve her vision.

The story of the horse Seabiscuit is another amazing account of seeing beyond appearances and holding fast to a vision. But it is more than that; it is the story of a man who could see past what everyone else saw: a lazy, difficult-to-train horse. Charles S. Howard saw the potential in this horse and had a vision of a champion. He took a washed-up jockey, a lost trainer and an undersized, knobby-kneed horse and created a team of winners.

He did not let the opinions of others deter him from what he knew was true. Because of his belief in and dedication to the image he had in his mind's eye, he kept taking the next right action toward cultivating the victor in the horse and in the people who were part of his story. In so doing, he created a dream that others could believe in and see for themselves.

Howard's dream became America's dream. The setting for the story was during the Great Depression, when people were desperate and without hope. They saw a horse that came from the same place they did, the back streets of nowhere, to transcend his perceived imperfections to defeat the pampered favorite.

Even his name, Seabiscuit, suggested hard times and poverty. It is another name for hardtack, the food that soldiers and sailors used in battle and at sea because of its simplicity and durability, when resources were scarce. Howard's vision of a winner was about more than his personal desire; he was also an inspiration for the common man and woman who had lost their optimism. People saw Seabiscuit succeeding and began to think that they, too, could crawl out of the despair they were in.

Who knows how many people were inspired enough by this story to begin to take steps toward recovering their own lives? When we follow our personal vision, we affect others in ways that we will never see, and it spreads like the mustard seed into the field of darkness and despair. And like the mustard plant, we discover a tenacity and hardiness that cannot be stopped, spreading nourishment and possibility into every corner of our beings. Little by little, our worlds begin to reflect what we know is true in our hearts.

Visions are born in the realm of the imagination. Glimpses of them can sprout up seemingly out of nowhere during times of quiet reflection, but only if the soil is prepared. That is why it is so important to give ourselves time to be still—so our imaginations can roam. Nighttime dreams are brimming with information. Our visions challenge us to look beyond the physical and the status quo and see the not so obvious.

In order to make our vision a reality, we begin to develop the God-like qualities that lie dormant in each of us, waiting to be shared. For example, we are all created with an unlimited capacity for compassion, generosity, creativity and ingenuity. Once we realize that we must develop these qualities in order to be successful, we discover gifts and talents we didn't know we had, and in sharing them, we also feel good about ourselves.

My story demonstrates this phenomenon. As I, along with many others, continued to build our church, I discovered a degree of confidence that I did not know I had. Being in a position of leadership, I had to take care of difficult situations that made me very uncomfortable. I often heard my voice shake and felt my knees wobble. But every time I faced my fears and took responsible action, I discovered a strength that had lain dormant within me, waiting for me to discover it.

For example, when we bought and renovated our building, I had no idea what it took to complete a construction project of that size. As the minister, I needed to address issues of timing and quality with contractors, even though I had no knowledge or skills in that area. I often felt afraid that people would see that I didn't know what I was talking about. Ultimately, I was afraid that I would harm the church in some way. Nevertheless, I spoke up, asked questions, made mistakes and held people accountable. As a result, I am much more confident in my abilities as a leader and minister.

As we develop our vision, hoarding our gifts becomes more and more difficult. Deep down, we all know what we are capable of. We have the potential for tremendous acts of greatness, even in the smallest and seemingly most inconspicuous encounters. When we have vision, we become more deliberate about expressing these qualities throughout the day.

People with vision are able to recognize these nudges and have the courage to act on them. They understand that the big picture materializes with each small step they take. Ultimately, they see that as they follow their vision, they become catalysts for change in their world. In turn, their lives take on a whole new meaning. Their life's purpose becomes an extension of their vision.

Seeing our path clearly also leads to better choices about where we spend our time. Those things that drain our energy become more obvious. When we have a clear vision about the direction of our lives, we are less likely to be distracted—even as we face the inevitable obstacles along the way.

A clear vision also creates purposeful action. We begin the process with enthusiasm, and our imagination soars as we entertain all of the possibilities—because, after all, we live in the field of infinite possibilities. We remain energized even when we're dealing with life's details, because it is attention to the next right thing that brings vision alive.

I once heard a story about three stonemasons building a cathedral, and each of them had very different perspectives about the ultimate purpose of their work. The first stonemason, when asked the nature of his task, answered, "I am laying stones." The second stonemason answered, "I am building a wall." In contrast, the third stonemason responded, "I am building a cathedral to the glory of God."

All three men were doing the same repetitive job. Yet it was the third man who went about his daily routine with joy and purpose because his actions were couched in vision.

Vision is also what propels us as we deal with the challenging conversations and decisions that arise when change is under way.

In 2008 the cable channel HBO aired a miniseries about John Adams, our second president, based on the book *John Adams* by David McCullough. It gave a realistic view of what our forefathers faced when laying the foundation for our country. So often history presents a romanticized view of that time period, with heroic stories and rousing songs of midnight rides. These accounts often neglect to tell the real tales of extreme sacrifices and hardships that just about everyone was experiencing. They knew that eventually they would break ties with their homeland and that their actions might result in war. There was also no consensus on how to realize their dream.

But they had a vision of a free and equal country. This dream's time had come, and it was going to be born through this group of courageous people in that moment. The dream they shared carried them when they thought they could not take another step.

Jesus was faced with the same difficult decision—of following his dream or playing it safe—on a daily basis. There is a story in the Bible that tells of the time Mary and Jesus' brothers arrived where he was teaching to fetch him home. It was a pivotal moment for Jesus. Effectively, they were asking him to give up his life's purpose and come home with them in order to avoid the unwanted attention he was getting because of his radical and dangerous message. They loved him dearly and were concerned for his safety.

Jesus was aware of the peril he was placing himself in by continuing his work. He understood the motives of his family, but he could not turn his back on what he knew was his soul's purpose. He knew his vision of the kingdom of heaven was greater than any one person or life. So instead of gathering his things and going home with his mother, he looked around and claimed that everyone in the room was his family. He went even further and said that those who do the will of the Father are his brothers and sisters. Those are his true family.

We are all visionaries. The question is not whether we have a vision; it is whether we pay attention to it. Vision comes in a variety of forms, and it comes to all of us. Having a vision and following it takes a tremendous amount of courage and fortitude. It means that you are looking to change the status quo. You see something different from what others see, and you dare to pursue it.

When we look at history and the roll call of heroes who have pursued their vision, we see how many of them acted like Jesus, with great courage and conviction, often in the face of extreme opposition. Dr. Martin Luther King Jr., with his dream of all races living together in harmony, picked up the baton that Jesus had handed off 2,000 years before. Dr. King spoke it, lived it and acted on it. Like Jesus, he knew that he was putting himself in danger with the words he was saying. He even had a premonition that if he did not stop, he would be assassinated. Yet he could not be stopped.

Dr. King is just one among many other heroes who were ridiculed, banished, persecuted and sometimes killed for their bold visions and new possibilities. Galileo was placed under house arrest for claiming that the earth was not the center of the universe. Even the threat of death could not stop his vision of greater knowledge of the universe. When it is time for something greater to be born, the idea will find a clear channel. It will come through someone who cannot turn away from the truth it carries, regardless of the repercussions.

What Did Jesus Do?

As you can see, following a vision is not for the faint of heart. Our vision for our lives is not simply a remedy to cure us of the surface dissatisfaction we may feel from time to time. Following our vision is certainly not meant to fix boredom. It is not the fleeting pursuit of pleasure that so many of us engage in, hoping that a particular activity or person will fulfill a need.

Vision is born from the pool of unfulfilled potential that resides in each of us and in every situation. It is a persistent nagging that will continue until we begin to take steps to realize it. Vision creates the possibility that every moment is a holy experience. This potential encompasses all realms of expression: physical, emotional, mental and spiritual.

And so it was with Jesus. He had foresight into the best that humanity could be. His vision was for us to know who we are. Let's put into context what he did and stood for.

He was born into a time when people suffered great oppression under Roman domination. The Israelites were a conquered people, tired and poor. Jesus not only saw his brothers and sisters suffering but could also relate to it because he experienced it.

Marcus Borg wrote in *Meeting Jesus Again for the First Time* how biblical scholars believe that Jesus was born into one of the lowest levels of Jewish society. The Gospels depict Joseph, his father, as a carpenter, which had a different connotation then than it does today. When a man was forced to work with his hands, Borg explained, it usually meant that he had lost his land and lived just beyond the reach of abject poverty.[2]

There were probably days when the holy family was not sure where their next meal would come from and nights they spent wondering whether they would have enough to pay both the Roman tax and the temple tax so that they would not be thrown out on the street. This is what Jesus experienced as he scanned the landscape of his culture, and it inspired a dream deep within him. Something in Jesus awoke as he grew up, causing him to form a different idea of what life was supposed to be.

Instead of turning outward and raging against conditions or resigning himself to an existence of silent suffering, Jesus turned inward, seeking a deeper relationship with God. He began by becoming familiar with the Hebrew Bible. There is an account of Jesus in the temple as a boy discussing those verses with teachers and holy men. Even at the tender age of 12, Jesus exhibited great insight into the familiar sacred text. This vast and intimate knowledge reflected a greater understanding than anyone had ever shown before. This laid the groundwork for his unprecedented relationship with God.

Jesus and his contemporaries did not see the world through the same set of lenses. To him God was personal, intimate, loving, nurturing and life-sustaining. He knew God as both a Father and Mother figure, and he knew that we are born from the Mind of God. He understood that God is the giver and the sustainer of life. Jesus saw himself as the Divine Son of God, heir to all that God is, and he saw the same thing for those around him at the time and for all of us to come. Jesus wanted us to be introduced to ourselves and the reality of who we are as sons and daughters of the One Mind.

From this awareness of himself and all of humankind, he began to formulate a vision of what life would be if we really knew this about ourselves. From his personal experience of God, he created a vision for each of us that is beyond anything that anyone had imagined up to that point.

Once Jesus was on fire with his vision, he dedicated his life to living it. That became the whole purpose for his existence. We can see that his every act and thought was predicated on manifesting his vision.

His descriptions of the kingdom of heaven do not describe a place; nor does he give instructions on how to get there. Instead he shrouds it in metaphors and parables. It is almost as though he is speaking in code and it is up to us to unravel its mysteries. His message of heaven becomes clearer as we grow and evolve spiritually.

Jesus' vision may seem to be beyond our reach, yet can you catch a glimpse of what he wanted us to see? Can you imagine a world in which every man, woman and child has enough to eat, a place to sleep, a sense of value and worth? Can you imagine a world in which people put one another's needs ahead of profit and productivity? Can you imagine a world in which sickness is a distant memory and people live joyous, fulfilled lives? This may sound a bit Pollyanna-ish, but I believe that this is what Jesus meant when he talked about the kingdom of heaven.

Jesus understood that his purpose was to introduce us to ourselves so that we, too, would know that we are valuable. Everything he did directed our attention back to the central theme of the kingdom of heaven, or the potential for the Divine in each of us.

He first knew this for himself. We can see by the statements he made about himself, in the Gospel of John, that he identified himself with his divinity. He tells us in 6:51, "I am the living bread that came down from heaven." In 8:12: "I am the light of the world. Whoever follows me will never walk in darkness." And in 15:1, "I am the true vine, and my Father is the vinegrower." These are all statements of vision and purpose. He saw himself as God's reality. It came alive in the psyche of his being. He then dedicated his life to manifesting his vision. This became his purpose.

When we have a clearly defined vision, our lives and everything about them take on a whole new meaning. No longer are we living to survive. Rather, we see how our actions and presence make a difference in the world. We are willing to do things that we normally would not do. We learn to hear and trust our inner guidance.

Everything we do is now measured according to how it helps us bring our vision to life. We have something that propels us forward and keeps us moving toward the dream. We have dedicated ourselves to something much bigger than we are. And so our lives change. A sense of well-being and fulfillment happens when we know that we will never be satisfied by compulsively scurrying around from person to person or place to place, grasping for something that is not there. Jesus showed us how to live in a way that would reap the results we were looking for.

Psychologist and theologian Thomas Moore, in his book *Care of the Soul*, talks about how so many of his clients acknowledge feeling empty and without purpose. They have disconnected from what he calls soul, or a sense of the sacred.[3] When we have lost our sense of what is holy and good in one another and life, we drift. Life has no meaning, and it becomes a series of acts motivated by a vain search for some sort of satisfaction.

But this all changes when we catch a glimpse of what Jesus taught about the kingdom of heaven and our part in it. As we stand with him and see a glimpse of his vision of the kingdom here on earth, something deep within us recognizes it as a possibility, and we become willing to dedicate everything in order to see it come to pass.

So join me, and together we will begin to hear and follow the vision that God designed for our lives.

Practicing the Practice

Spend time visioning. The foundation for this process was introduced to me by a number of different ministers over the years.

1. Begin by entering into a meditative state. Once you have set aside the distractions of the day and quieted your mind, begin to ask the following questions: *What is God's highest idea for me and those around me? What does the kingdom of heaven look and feel like?* Make it personal. Bring it down to the smallest detail of your life. Remember, this is not about earning something in the far-off future. This is

about cooperating with God to create heaven right where you are standing.

Let Holy Spirit take your imagination to places you never dreamed of, where you have a sense that the impossible is possible. Let your mind take you there now. If you see it, then it is the desire of the Universe to be made manifest through you. This is your vision of heaven on earth, and as you claim it, it will then become the very purpose of your existence.

2. Write it down, taste it, feel what it would be like if it were really true. Hear the sounds and see the picture clearly. Write it, draw it, dance it.

3. Then ask, *What part do I play in making it happen?* Spend time with this idea. Don't let the possibility of it scare you off. Document it, and then read it to a trusted friend before you let your "common sense" take control again.

4. *Do not judge what comes to you!* Hear it without censoring. In the beginning, it may be that your vision is very materialistic. So many of us have been taught that it was wrong to want things, or that if something good happened to us, it meant that we had taken away someone else's good. Many of us have to start out by learning how to allow the "stuff" back into our lives. We can learn to trust that our basic needs will be taken care of and that we matter. Don't worry; you won't stay stuck here. You will move past the point of manipulating energy for your own good and will realize the contribution you were created to make.

5. Ask: *What kind of world do I see for my children and grand-children?* Native Americans have a tradition of looking at how their decisions will affect their children seven generations into the future. See how your immediate vision will contribute to the world in generations to come.

6. Make God big enough to realize your vision. Remind yourself that your vision is God's way of expressing into the universe more of everything that God is. Realize that there is no image too big or too grand for God. If you can imagine it, then it is possible. The potential is embedded in the very fabric of your being.

7. Share your vision with a trusted friend, yet be careful whom you share it with at this stage. It is a fragile, tender being, in need of protection. So share with those who will support you in your sacred endeavor. Even better, find someone who is following his or her own vision. If that nagging voice in your head tries to talk some "sense" into you, then thank your inner voice for sharing and continue with the task at hand. Let the entire breadth of your being take in the possibility of the kind of world your mind is depicting for you. Relish and revel in it. Because now the hard work begins.

Do Greater Things

Faith

Jesus believed in his vision. He had an unwavering faith in his image of how the world should be. His vision was as real as the air he breathed, and his faith moved his feet. Faith is the next prerequisite for replicating what Jesus did. It is both cause and effect, a spiritual discipline and a gift that we gain as we practice it.

Once again, let's start by turning to the dictionary for a working definition of faith. *Merriam-Webster's Collegiate Dictionary* defines it as "belief and trust," which seems simple enough. Expanding on this definition, having faith means believing that there will be a particular outcome as a result of some influence or act. We have faith that A + B = C. Consider a simple act that we perform every day.

Every morning when you brush your teeth, you go to the faucet ready to turn its handle and have water come gushing out. You don't wonder whether the faucet will deliver water. You simply trust that water will be there as it has been every other time you performed the same ritual.

Jesus wanted us to understand that the flow of God is as reliable as water from our faucet. It is not dependent on any act of ours other than a turn of the handle. This is the kind of unquestioning faith that he had in God, and he knew that if we were going to repeat what he did, then we needed the same type of faith.

Think about it: We don't get up in the morning and pray to our faucet for water. We don't tell our faucet that we will be "good" today to ensure its steady stream. We don't ask forgiveness from the faucet for our misdeeds. Yet we do these things, hoping to find favor with God.

Faith is an expectation. We expect certain things in life based on what we have come to see as normal. We become so used to conditions that we don't question whether they can be or should be any different. Our expectation becomes as automatic as breathing, and it seems heresy to question things or to assume anything different.

Jesus radically challenged this practice. He knew that as long as we had faith in the limiting ideas that we believed were normal, we would never evolve to the point of being able to repeat what he did. He wanted us to break down the barriers we place around ourselves—barriers that keep God's goodness from us—so that we could expand our idea of normal to include his vision of a rich, abundant life. He knew that this meant shattering our worn-out assumptions about life.

Imagine a New Normal

Most of us have become so conditioned to suffering that we believe it is normal, along with illness, deprivation and a sense of isolation. But Jesus had a different view of how the world worked. He wanted us to understand that we always have the power to expand our definition of what is acceptable. That is where faith coupled with vision comes in. Because we have faith in a loving, all-sustaining God, we can start entertaining a different concept—even in the face of bleak circumstances and seemingly insurmountable odds.

Before any of us can make changes in our lives, we must have faith. Once we recognize that there is more to life than the hardship to which we have resigned ourselves, we begin to see that life can be good. We realize that the pain and suffering we experience may be the facts in the moment, but they don't have to be our standard.

I'm reminded of the time I spent working as a speech pathologist. One of the things I did in that role was to help hearing-impaired children get accustomed to hearing aids. I will never forget the looks on their faces when we put the aids in their ears for the first time. The children's eyes would light up, and they would often squeal with delight. For them, muffled and distorted sounds were the norm; but with technology, we changed their norm. Their world expanded as a result, and they discovered a new hearing standard.

Jesus wanted his listeners to discover a new standard of awareness too. He wanted them to entertain the possibility that they were packed with power to change their circumstances. He longed for the people around him to see that as they turned to God, God would provide them with all that they needed. They were not at the mercy of the world around them. Just because certain conditions were the norm did not mean they were meant to stay that way forever.

The evidence of our ability to broaden what is accepted practice abounds. For example, during Jesus' time, if someone contracted leprosy, he or she was condemned to a painful life and an equally painful death. Lepers were banished from the community because leprosy was thought to be a highly contagious disease. That norm changed as we grew in our understanding of the disease, how it spreads, and ways to prevent and cure it. Today we are appalled at the thought of treating someone that way. But it is not because somehow we are better people; rather, because of new information, we have been able to change the status quo.

In order for our own definition of what is normal to evolve, we must cultivate a perspective, which means a paradigm shift in our image of, and relationship with, God. Having the faith of Jesus means rooting out the mythical idea of God as a man in the sky, deciding whose prayers will be answered or not, and "replacing it," in the words of minister, writer and educator Gene Marshall, with the experience of God as the "ground of all being." Marshall was quoted by Rev. Michael Dowd, an evolutionary evangelist, in *Thank God for Evolution*, which also quoted him as saying, "God is that awesome and mysterious Reality in which all things live and move and have their being, and out of which all things live and move and have their being, and out of which all things emerge and into which all things return."[1]

In the aforementioned book, Dowd wrote about how we see the world as we see God, and we see God as we see the world. He said, "All religious stories, metaphors, and spiritual beliefs are true in this sense: They are true to a people's experience of the world." He went on to say, "If we imagine God as beautiful, gracious, loving, awesome, power-ful, majestic, or faithful, it is because we have known or experienced beauty, grace, love, awe, power, majesty, or trust-worthiness in the world."[2]

This statement can also be reversed. If we see God as harsh and demanding, then the world will seem harsh and demanding. In later chapters, I address in more detail the process of changing your image of God. For now, simply be willing to take a look at how you see God and your relation-ship to God. Be willing to question what you expect from God, and observe how that plays out in your life.

Many of us believe that the problems in our world come from a lack of faith. We talk about doing this or that in order to gain more faith, as if we were defective. We believe that if we have the right amount of faith, God will hear us and we will be able to influence him to give us what we want. So faith becomes something to obtain in order to please God so that he will do what we ask for. Faith becomes a bargaining chip.

Life Journeys

Believe it or not, we have all the faith we need. Changing our norm is not a matter of gaining more faith; it is a matter of shifting where we have placed our faith. What we focus on grows. The things we focus on then become our normal.

Just watch the news one evening and see if this is not true. Watch your response as you listen to how the reporters present their stories. Pay attention to your body as you react to the tone of their voices and the language they use. Then observe what in your environment catches your attention afterward.

As I write this, our country is in a deep economic recession. Reports of unemployment, house foreclosures and financial hardship fill the airwaves. I find that the more I listen, the more I notice the closed businesses and empty storefronts. As a result, I feel myself becoming frightened by the possibility of losing everything, even as I sit in my comfortable home wanting for nothing.

This is not to diminish the very real suffering that people are experiencing. But the more we focus on that aspect, the more it becomes our normal, and the more we will perpetuate it. I recently heard former president Bill Clinton share how we don't need more bad news about how bad it is going to get; we need a cheerleader who will reassure us that we will be okay. We need someone to hold out the possibility of something very different from what we are experiencing right now. That is what faith does for us.

Think about how you drive a car. When you direct your attention to something on the road, the car naturally heads in that direction. Whether you mean to or not, you steer the car toward the direction of your focus. Faith steers our lives according to where we have placed our attention.

Our assumptions about life also act as the container for what we can receive. Our assumptions define where we place our faith. If we see ourselves a certain way, then no matter how hard we try, we cannot change the shape or size of the container of our lives.

Unity minister and writer Eric Butterworth, in his book *Spiritual Economics*, told the story of a salesman who could not generate above a certain income, regardless of the circumstance. When the company hired him, it had placed him in one of the best territories, but he did only $25,000 in commissions, when he should easily have gotten $75,000. Not wanting to fire the man, his manager put him in the poorest area. The salesman again earned $25,000, which was considered remarkable for that area. The manager reassigned his employee to a great territory once again, believing that the salesman had turned himself around—but to everyone's dismay, the salesman got the same results he had the year before in the low-performing area. He saw himself as a $25,000-a-year salesman and could not rise above that income level.[3]

We do that in a million different ways in our own lives. We set the limit and say that the limit is the way things are. We have unquestionable faith in whatever limit we have placed on ourselves, and as a result, we rarely go beyond that limit. This could apply to any area of our lives. We have limits for money, for health, for jobs, for relationships, for happiness. But Jesus came to help us tear down our walls of limitation so that we could see and have faith in the field of infinite possibility.

Are We Manifesting Faith?

To develop this new faith focus, we must change the way we see the world. We must expand what we think is possible for ourselves and others. Jesus' example challenges us to do this, and, believe it or not, it is much easier than you think. It is simply a matter of shifting our focus away from the evidence that says the world is dangerous and life is hard to the proof that God's good is active and everywhere present.

As our focus moves from what we don't want to what we desire, we become excited at what could be. We begin to imagine something different for ourselves and others, and we begin to feel the tiny seeds of faith in that possibility take root and grow within us. As a result, we begin to experience peace and a deep sense of well-being, and ultimately, more of what we want manifests in our outer world. We learn to trust in life's abundance as we notice the abundance that is already right in front of us.

Our thoughts and words are the clues showing us where our faith—where our confidence—is. We may think we have trust in God, but our conversations with others and ourselves may tell a different story. Listen, for example, to how often you talk about being worried that you won't be able to pay the bills when your checkbook balance is low.

Many of us profess to have faith that God will provide, yet in the wee hours of the morning, we find ourselves wide awake, panicking about how we are going to find the money for rent, utilities or medical insurance. If we look closely enough, we can see how our conversations reveal a faith in a god that withholds things from us. We are afraid that it is God's will for us to suffer and struggle for some perverted reason.

Jesus encourages us to believe otherwise by noticing that the world was created with the means to support life built into it. The full potential of God is present in every moment and circumstance. How could it be otherwise? In Genesis 1:1 we read, "In the beginning God ..." (NIV). This is probably one of the most profound and powerful statements in the Bible. In fact, the rest of the Bible wouldn't really be necessary if we ever truly came to understand the impact of those four simple words.

If it is true that there was only God in the beginning, then everything that was created was made from the substance of God. There was no raw material for God to use during the creative process other than itself. If that is the case, then the nature of God is built into everything.

Stay with me in this line of thinking. We believe, don't we, that God is whole—and is therefore incapable of creating anything that is less than complete? If that is true, then the universe was designed to express abundance and affluence because it reflects the nature of God. Embedded in every idea and life form is what it needs to grow and flourish.

We are an idea conceived in the mind of God. And as ideas, we are complete. From the beginning, our fullness was present in the mind of God. But it is up to us to unlock this potential and bring it alive in the routine of our lives. As we start to recognize our potential and have faith in our unlimited possibility, our focus shifts from what we think can't happen to what we know is possible. When we have faith in the *allness* of God, we come to expect life to be rich and fulfilling. That becomes our new norm.

That is what Jesus showed us over and over again. With every act of healing or apparent miracle, he gave us the evidence of God's sustaining love, and the substance on which we learn to depend. He showed us that our faith is well placed when we turn our attention away from the appearance of scarcity and focus instead on the all-prevailing presence and flow of God.

I'm reminded of a television program I watched recently in which a character was playing the president of the United States. During negotiations with another country, she made the comment, "You will have the full power of the United States military backing you." Knowing that the full capacity of God backs and supports our every move, our faith is directed toward God and away from any appearance of limitation.

Paul told us in Hebrews 11:1, "Faith is the assurance of things hoped for, the conviction of things not seen." We learn to go beyond what we experience with the five senses and instead look to the invisible realm of Spirit.

What Did Jesus Do?

Jesus had this kind of faith. He knew that the abundance God intends for our lives is as dependable as the earth's support for the seeds it receives. In Mark 4:1-8, he presented the analogy of planting the seed into the ground. He related what happened to the seed that fell on rocky and shallow soil: It had no place to plant roots, so it withered away. But then, "Other seed fell into good soil and brought forth grain, growing up and increasing and yielding thirty and sixty and hundredfold." We can't see how it happens, but nevertheless, once in the earth and properly attended to, the seed grows into the stalk, the head and then the full grain in the head. Given the right conditions, everything can go through this cycle.

My husband and I planted our spring garden this morning. With faith, we went to the farmer's co-op to purchase our seeds. We then tilled the garden, scattered organic fertilizer and mapped out where each vegetable would go. After all of the preparation, we sowed the seeds. We were willing to put the time and effort into planting because we had enough faith that the seeds would produce what the package described, and that in a few short months we would harvest our vegetables.

Jesus tended his fields of heaven. The vision he had for himself and each of us determined what he believed was possible, and he had enough faith in his dream to give it the necessary attention. Through his actions and teachings, he planted the seeds of his dream into our collective consciousness. And ever since, humankind has felt the stirrings of a new heaven and earth, and as a species we have continued to grow toward that idea.

Specifically, Jesus had faith in humanity as the living expression of Spirit and was willing to invest time and energy in those he met in order to help them realize their divine identity. No one was exempt from his teachings and presence, because he knew that all people had the seeds of unlimited possibility planted into their very being.

John 4:7-26 tells this tender lesson in the tale of Jesus and the Samaritan woman by the well. According to the story, Jesus arrived at the well at noon and asked the woman for a cup of water.

Now, let me stop there and explain why this simple request for water was so radical. For one thing, the woman was a Samaritan, a member of one of the lost tribes of Israel. The Samaritans had been conquered several centuries earlier and were assimilated into other cultures until they were no longer considered pure according to Jewish standards of the time. In addition, the woman was going for water in the middle of the day, indicating that she did not want to be seen by others. She was living with a man who was not her husband, which seemed to be a pattern for her. Because she was an outcast, she had to wait until everyone else had drawn water, so even if she was able to get any water, it would be tepid.

And so it was this outcast whom Jesus, a respected teacher and rabbi, asked for water. As he began talking with her, he did what came naturally to him as someone dedicated to living his vision. He started to teach about the nature of God. He planted the seeds of a different life into her parched heart. He did this because he saw something in her that nobody else saw.

He gave her a message of faith, hope and love. He described God as Spirit and compared God to the wind. He emphasized that God is always there, and even though she couldn't see God, if she had eyes to see and ears to hear, she would find proof of God all around her, just as she saw evidence of the wind.

This message reverberates today. We come to know God and to develop faith in God's power and presence by paying attention to the evidence of that presence all around us. In awe, we acknowledge the seemingly invisible hand that arranges things in ways that are beyond anything we could have imagined.

Miracles Then and Now

Jesus lived his faith in everything he did. His life demon-strated the power of focused faith in action. As a result, those around him were so transformed by his presence that they told larger-than-life stories about him.

One such tale involved the miracle of the fish and loaves, which we will explore in more depth in Chapter 6, on grati-tude. This event was so huge in the minds of the people at the time that it made its way into three of the four Gospels. According to the written accounts, Jesus was literally able to produce something from thin air. It was as though the bread and fish had been as vapor, waiting for someone to gather all the pieces together to give them form and definition.

People have tried to explain the phenomenon of these larger-than-life accounts. Eric Butterworth, in *Spiritual Economics*, shared how George Lamsa, translator of the Aramaic Bible, presented a theory suggesting that right when Jesus was giving thanks, during the manifestation process, wagons of supplies showed up with enough food to feed the crowds of people.

Lamsa suggested that the needed supplies came from a merchant in town who was unable to attend the event and wanted to do something to support Jesus' efforts. It could have happened this way; no one knows for sure. Regardless of the means, however, something spectacular certainly occurred.[4]

This story demonstrates the combined power of vision and faith. If we look at the anatomy of a miracle, we first have to ask, "What did Jesus expect from that moment? What was his normal?" Jesus had faith in God as abundance. He could see the evidence of infinite supply all around him and expected it to be made manifest at that moment to fulfill his hunger. He understood that when God breathed life into his nostrils, the Universe was already prepared to support his daily needs. In that instant, Jesus expected to be fed.

He never questioned whether the Power that had created him with these physical needs would *not* give him what he needed in order to live life easily. What a cruel creator that would be! He knew only a friendly Universe, in which it was intended that every man, woman and child would have his or her basic requests met. The focus of his attention was on the supply of the Universe as evidenced by the five fish and two loaves of bread.

Although we will never know what happened that day, we do know, according to the stories, that people left the hillside nourished in mind, body and spirit.

Greg Mortenson, founder and director of the Central Asia Institute and co-author of *Three Cups of Tea*, performed a similar modern-day miracle. While mountain climbing in Pakistan, he found himself lost and near death while descending a summit in one of the world's most remote corners. He wandered, barely alive, into a village, where he was nursed back to life. During his recovery, he began to notice his surroundings and saw how the children of the village had no place to learn. The girls in particular were forgotten, but their hunger for knowledge could not be extinguished. He watched as the girls would file out to a field with sticks to write crude words in the dirt as they recited the alphabet.

Mortenson believed in these young girls' intrinsic value. He saw potential in them and knew that he had to do something to feed their minds and develop their abilities. He also saw the connection between ignorance, prejudice and the creation of enemies. As a result, he was enlivened by the dream that these girls could develop and become agents for good. He understood that in order for this to happen, the entire village would have to adopt a new paradigm regarding their children, especially the girls. Mortenson pledged that he would return to the village to help build them a school.

Once back in the States, he had no idea how he was going to fulfill that promise. At the time, he was living out of his car and working as an emergency room nurse. But he had faith in a God that wanted all of his children to be educated. Mortenson managed to get folks interested in his project, and a year later, after lots of hard work and mistakes along the way, he was able to return and build that school.

The story does not stop there. Because of Mortenson's vision and faith in himself and the people he wanted to assist, his idea captivated others. Wealthy patrons backed his enterprise and helped him form a foundation. According to his online biography, he has built more than 90 schools to date, in some of the most isolated and religiously fundamentalist areas of Afghanistan and Pakistan.[5]

His vision of peace through education continues to grow. Because of his faith in the young children of that remote village as ambassadors for peace, more and more schools are being built, filling the minds of impressionable young children with visions of something new and life-affirming.

Healing From the Source

Healing was another area in which Jesus demonstrated unwavering belief in the power and presence of God. So often when we are sick, we pray to God for help. We hope that if we pray hard enough and use the right words, we can persuade God to do something that "he" might not otherwise do. Again, Jesus didn't have faith in this kind of God; he had faith in a principled God and knew that certain laws were always at work, particularly the law of wholeness and health. So when the sick approached him for healing, he didn't see them as broken; he saw them as they were created to be, vital and complete. As a result, they began to see themselves the same way. They mirrored his expectation, and so their bodies were restored to wholeness.

Because of his absolute faith in God as principle, he was able to convey this same certainty to others. His faith in the vision of the kingdom of heaven touched something deep within the people who sought him for healing. They resonated with his teachings because they knew that those teachings were true. As a result of their association with him, these people were also able to shift the focus of their faith toward health and away from sickness.

This was a key point in Jesus' teachings. For him, it was imperative that people understood that the same healing power available to him was available to everyone. We read repeatedly how Jesus told people that it was not he, their teacher, who did the healing; rather, it was their faith that made them well.

He did not want his listeners to depend on him to manifest the kingdom of God. They would never live up to what they were capable of if they needed him to perform acts. If they were going to bring that kingdom alive on a mass scale, then they must see for themselves what he knew to be true. So Jesus directed people toward the evidence of the kingdom of heaven all around them until they could experience it for themselves.

Myrtle Fillmore, co-founder of the Unity movement, repeated this same brand of faith when she was healed from a terminal illness. After receiving a diagnosis that gave her only six months to live, she attended a lecture and heard the affirmation, "I am a child of God, therefore I do not inherit sickness."

When she heard this statement, every cell in her body responded to what it knew was true. She spent the next two years working with this statement, increasing her faith that wholeness was her natural state. As she continued to work with this principle in mind, her body reflected that vision, and she was healed.

The story continues. Other people began to notice what was happening to Fillmore, and they asked her to pray for them as well. They were certain that she had special healing powers. But Fillmore knew otherwise. She was a devout student of her master teacher, Jesus, and knew that the power of healing lay in each person. So instead of praying for them, she directed them toward their own innate healing powers.

In *Healing Letters*, a collection of prayer letters she wrote to those asking for her help, she shared, "As you learn to see the fullness of God's life and love and power and substance in others, you will know that you need not pour out your own for them. You will have the knowledge and the light to call their attention to what they have and prompt them to use it."[7]

This process takes imagination, which is simply the ability to see beyond appearances. Jesus had that ability. He had the power to picture what he knew to be true in the face of dire circumstances suggesting otherwise. He could see beyond those situations and hold firm to the possibility of life that was available in each moment. And people were healed of their afflictions when they came into contact with him. But he said over and over again that it was their faith that made them well.

The story in Mark of the woman who touched the hem of Jesus' garment is another powerful example of faith and determination. She had been bleeding for years, and there was nothing any of the doctors could do to stop it. She heard about this man Jesus and knew that if she could just touch his garment, then she would be made whole.

She fought the crowds that were pushing in around him and forced her way to him. When she touched his garment, he immediately felt the power flow from him into her and asked who had touched him. She confessed, terrified that she had done something wrong. But he blessed her and told her that it was her faith that had made her whole. It was the image she had in her mind of the possibility of wholeness, and the idea that she would be restored to health simply by being in his presence, that had stopped the bleeding. Jesus did not heal her; he held the image of wholeness for her until she knew it for herself.

We have this same power of imagination to see things as they can be. As expressed in Paul's statement, "Faith is ... the conviction of things not seen," faith activated is imagination in action. We put forth our power to imagine beyond what we can see and explain. Our imagination is the drawing board of our faith.

Dare to Dream

I don't think I missed an episode of the TV show *Lost in Space* when I was a child. The sets were crude, and the technology was almost laughable compared with today's standards. And yet we tuned in each week to watch the characters run from aliens and take directions from a talking robot. Our actions demonstrated the power of imagination.

Think how far we have come since the first space movies. The elementary ideas that were presented have morphed into powerful demonstrations of science that have allowed us to go where no one ever thought possible. I remember the first time I showed my third-grade class the pictures from the spaceship *Challenger* taken on the surface of Mars. From our classroom in Murfreesboro, Tennessee, we joined millions of other awestruck viewers from around the world who were exploring the actual landscape of Mars. It was a far cry from the imagined scenery depicted in those silly movies. And yet our ability to imagine the possibilities also bolstered our faith in our ability to realize those possibilities.

When you allow your imagination to roam, you dare to dream. You begin to conceive of what could be, and you begin to mold your life around it. You start to have faith in the possibility of your dreams, and you pursue them. That is why it is vital to have a powerful vision to pull you along.

Faith in something greater than ourselves means that we are less directed by our personal desires and are able to surrender more easily to the activity of God. Everything that Jesus did was meant to glorify God by showing the power and presence of God in each moment. Jesus could not have done for personal gain the things that he did. He would not have had the same incredible results. He had faith in the infinite substance of God and needed no personal recognition for what he did. He would have diminished his power and belief if he had needed the fame that comes with that kind of ability.

You, too, can have that kind of faith. As you commit to a spiritual practice, you begin to see how your faith shifts from believing the worst to knowing the best. As this process takes place, your role becomes clear. Your grip on a rigid view of life loosens, creating more room for the power of God to move through you. You develop faith that God is active and the things that Jesus promised just might be so. All things become possible.

So shift your faith. Begin to see the world as Jesus did, and entertain the idea that God's good is active and alive, and you are the way God comes alive in our world.

Practicing the Practice

1. Begin by paying attention to where you have placed your faith. When you find yourself faced with challenging situations and experience fear or anxiety, stop and ask yourself, *What do I believe about this situation and God right now? What do I expect?* Your fear will show you how you see God in that moment.

2. The next step is to begin to see God differently. God can bless you only to the extent that you let God do so. Begin to cultivate a feeling about God that nurtures a sense of well-being and trust inside you. You can't anger God or

make God go away by believing in something that will only draw you closer to her. You will do further work on your image of God in the next chapter on prayer. For now, just begin to play with a different idea of God.

3. Take an inventory of what you expect from life. What do you see as normal? When someone talks about having a cold, do you expect to contract it as well? When you listen to the news, do you presume the worst? What do you expect from other people and their treatment of you?

4. Another way of identifying what you expect from life is to make a list of your fears, which are actually your expectations of what will happen to you. The more aware you become of your unspoken fears, the more you can change them.

5. Once you have your list, create statements of affirmation for each fear that will help you trust God. Repeating simple statements of truth over and over again helps pry our attention from the chaos of the world and brings it back to the peace of the presence within. That is the power of a mantra or affirmation. You can simply repeat a word like *love* or *peace* to return your faith to God. "God is love," "God is my Source" and "God is here now" are powerful statements of truth that have worked for countless others. I encourage you to create your own statements that you can use to affirm the infinite presence of Spirit.

6. Begin to notice the evidence of God in your life. Begin to see those times when things do fall into place or when, out

of the blue, you have what you need at the exact time you need it. Many people keep gratitude journals. I invite you to keep an "evidence of God" journal or answered-prayer journal. Jesus had faith in God because he could see the evidence of God all around him, even in the midst of what appeared to be lack and deprivation. So pay attention. Take note. This will allow you to reach back and say to yourself, *The power of God was active in that situation, and it turned out in a way I never could have planned, so maybe I can trust that it will happen again.*

-4-

Prayer

Before we go on, let's revisit the purpose of this book. My intention is to help all of us believe that we have the same power Jesus had, and then to get on with the business of wielding that power. This isn't just my fanciful idea. Jesus' statement in John 14:12 ("Very truly, I tell you, the one who believes in me will also do the works that I do and, in fact, will do greater works than these, because I am going to the Father") told us that this is so. His words in the Gospels told us that we all have the power to repeat these same kinds of miraculous acts, and he urged us to get busy with the task at hand.

Let's look again at what Jesus wants us to repeat. When we study his example, we see that he performed extraordinary acts of compassion, generosity, power and wisdom. He fed the hungry, healed the sick, challenged the righteous and comforted the afflicted. Jesus knew that he was not defined or limited by his physical being.

He tapped into the wellspring of God's creative nature and was able to bring this understanding to bear in ways that dramatically changed people's lives. He knew that he was a channel through which the power of God was expressed, and his acts naturally demonstrated his awareness. He then called on each of us to discover how we, too, are the conduit for God. He knew that as we discovered our own innate glory for ourselves and shared it accordingly, more and more of us would experience heaven here on earth.

So how did Jesus grow his faith and vision? How did he discover and understand who he was? Jesus had a very simple way of tuning in to the realm of the Divine. He prayed.

Prayer was vital to Jesus. He talked about it continually, and he prayed often. The next time you read the New Testament, notice how often it mentions that Jesus prayed. The Bible tells us that he prayed all night, withdrew from the crowds to pray, went to the garden to pray, lifted his eyes to pray. It seems that he included prayer in every aspect of his life and ministry, and he made it a point to make sure that the people around him, particularly his disciples, knew when he was praying.

What Is Prayer?

What do we mean exactly when we use the word *prayer*? Father Thomas Keating, in *Open Mind, Open Heart*, said, "Contemplative prayer is the process of interior transformation, a conversation initiated by God, and leading, if we consent, to divine union."[1] Author, minister and therapist Wayne Muller, in *Learning to Pray*, described it as "deep faithful listening, waiting for what is hidden to be revealed. Prayer is not words, prayer is what happens when you listen and wait, beneath the words, for the outline of heaven to emerge."[2] Myrtle Fillmore said that prayer "lifts the individual into a wonderful sense of oneness with God, who is Spirit, the source of every good and perfect thing."[3]

Prayer is the time we spend fostering a relationship with the divine. It is the time we set aside, and the method we use, to gain a deeper understanding of who we are, who God is and who we are in relationship to God. Something within us knows there is more to our lives than what we can see on the surface, and we long to connect with the unseen Presence. Prayer is how we make that connection.

Jesus knew this. He understood that in order to experience the kingdom of heaven, he had to have a relationship with the Presence. Prayer led Jesus inward, where he discovered the truth about the nature of his being and his relationship to his Creator. As a result, Jesus saw only union between himself and God. As far as Jesus was concerned, there was no "me" and "you." He evolved to the point where, in seeing himself and others, he saw only God.

His awareness of his oneness with Spirit was only the beginning. He then translated this knowledge into action. He knew that God acted through and as him. He understood that others would come to know Ultimate Reality through him and that he would be God's standard-bearer.

Jesus' profound understanding of and rich experience with prayer could not have happened if he had used the traditional method of praying. He did not beseech God; he did not pray to get God to do something. He prayed to know God, pure and simple. His sole intention in prayer was to realize union with his Creator.

His example challenges us to examine the manner in which we pray. So often we pray to a god outside us to save us from life's hardships or to intervene for us when we are faced with difficulties. This method of prayer creates some real problems and inconsistencies if you examine the ideology behind it.

Recently, my town was hit with a series of tornadoes. There was one in particular that ripped through the center of town, destroying everything it touched along the way. You could see the general path it took when you looked at the aerial shots, but even that was erratic. One house would be destroyed, while the one next door stood untouched. Two people were killed and several injured.

One comment I often heard was how people had prayed to God to spare them from the devastation and keep them safe. When they emerged and saw that they were all right, they let out a huge sigh of relief and gave thanks that their prayers had been answered.

Now, on the surface this seems like a perfectly normal reaction, but if we dig a bit deeper, we find a view of a god that is selective and maybe even capricious. It suggests that God will listen to some prayers and ignore or deny others. It implies that his response to our prayers is as unpredictable as the tornado.

I think about the woman and her 9-week-old baby who were killed during the storm. I am sure that she was praying harder than she ever had before, but it would seem that it was to no avail. Did God find her prayers unacceptable? Had she done something to deserve to die in such a way?

I can feel you recoil from this thought as you read this, and so you should. But in fact, this is the underlying belief that drives our petitions of prayer. Those of you reading this book may not literally burn your best lamb, but you still think getting your prayers answered is contingent on saying or doing the right thing.

The truth is that we live in a chaotic, ever-changing world in which we are vulnerable to weather patterns and the actions of others. None of us is immune to life's difficulties. We have all experienced loss, hardship and illness. Our lives and the world we've created—a world where negative things happen—are finite. It is built into the design. Even Jesus was crucified.

So Jesus prayed not to be spared from life's challenges but to know how to be fully present for them in a way that would allow him to evolve into more of the man he was meant to be.

∞

He never flinched from what life brought him. Instead he saw each challenge as an opportunity to demonstrate God greater. His faith in the allness of God was far mightier than any circumstance, and his prayers reflected his awareness of that truth. On the flip side, his prayers gave him strength to meet his challenges with grace and dignity.

Prayer puts us in touch with what is true. As a result, we change the way we act. We learn to be more present and more loving. We tap into an infinite source of strength and wisdom, which allows this goodness to become our reality. And our lives do become better, but not because we have pleased God and he has decided to bless us. Rather, we have brought forth the potential for something better that is available to everyone.

That is why, if you are going to replicate what Jesus did, you must scrutinize and change your prayer life. If you listen closely, you will hear how many of us pray with a catch in our voice. We pray believing that we are at God's mercy, and we don't always trust that God will have mercy on us. Effectively, we pray hoping and disbelieving at the same time, all the while feeling helpless, dependent and vulnerable.

It comes down to this: We don't really believe that God's will for us is good. We wonder whether it's appropriate to believe that God's abundance is our abundance or God's wholeness is our wholeness. We have developed the misguided belief that a god outside us will decide whether we deserve a good life. And when disasters like the tornado happen, we often label the results "God's will." God either meant the tornado to hit the house or not. This "benevolent" power outside us decides our lives, and that is that.

Life Journeys

Recently, during a luncheon I was having with friends, the topic of God's will came up. The conversation beautifully illustrated our misconception of divine will. Some of the women described how they prayed to accept challenges as God's will. They prayed to accept that God never gave them more than they could handle.

As they talked, I had this image of God up in heaven with a pain-tolerance meter assigned to each of us. I could see him walking to each person's meter and saying, "This person can stand a bit more suffering; let me pour it on." I did not contribute to the conversation, but I thought to myself, *No wonder people turn away from God. It is scary to pray "Your will be done" if it could possibly mean that God wants catastrophe for me. I would rather lay low and hope that God does not notice me.*

I used to pray that way. I used to pray in hopes that God would pay attention to me and grant my wishes. At the same time, I was afraid to call attention to myself, because I was sure that his will for me meant the worst: suffering and hardship as the way to a holier life. I certainly did not believe that I had a right to expect happiness and fulfillment. The more I suffered, the more acceptable I was to God, according to my broken perception. So for me, prayer was an exercise in futility.

I also felt that I didn't have a right to pray. I felt torn because I knew it was something I was supposed to do, according to my teachers, but I didn't feel worthy to take God's attention away from things that really mattered. So prayer was also a source of great confusion for me. On the one hand it was an obligation, something I did to avoid incurring the wrath of God. And on the other hand, it meant that I was depriving someone else of God's favor and attention.

I was also convinced that prayer was not something that would work for me. I wasn't acceptable enough to God for him to grant my wishes. I just knew I had to clean up my act before I could go to God. My dress had to be ironed and my hair combed before I could be granted an audience with "the Father." And never mind the soil that I believed was on my soul! I assumed that I would spend the rest of eternity making up for what I considered to be my sins and failings.

I do not believe that my experience is unique. In fact, I would venture to guess that many of you have had very similar experiences. Jesus knew this. He knew that many of the people around him did not see prayer as a way to know God greater. This grieved him deeply, and he wanted to change this for people. He wanted them to have the same kind of deep, mystical connection with the divine that he had. That is why he talked about prayer so frequently. He knew that if we changed how we prayed, we, too, would come to know Spirit better. We would experience God firsthand and would thereby learn to recognize ourselves as the heirs to the kingdom of heaven.

In order for all of this to come to pass, our image of God must change. We must relinquish the God of punishment, along with the crazy idea that we have to do something to get God to deliver our wish list. In addition, and most important, we must learn a different language to use with God.

This is the kind of prayer that Jesus taught. He showed us that prayer is the way we discover and realize God. It is how we connect with the divine in order to allow it to be expressed through us unimpeded.

What Did Jesus Do?

Jesus saw God very differently from the way others around him saw God. Instead of a god of vengeance, Jesus talked about a god of love. He referred to God as *Abba*, which translates "father" or "papa" and used images of God that suggest a maternal as well as a paternal love. He talked about God knowing the number of hairs on our head and caring about whether the sparrows had enough to eat. If God was concerned about these things, then how could God not be concerned about our needs?

As we pray in this new way modeled for us by Jesus, we change the way we see God and remove "him" from the limited container in which we've placed "him." We no longer see ourselves at the mercy of God; nor do we see God as a glorified Santa Claus. The very nature of our relationship with God changes at the core, preparing us to replicate what Jesus did. Prayer becomes the vehicle through which we discover the potential for wholeness and expansion that lies at the heart of every situation and within each of us. We then dedicate ourselves in our prayer life to bringing this potential alive.

Some of the most powerful statements that Jesus made, such as "The Father and I are one," affirmed for him what he knew to be true, that there was no separation between him and God. His prayers demonstrated that he knew God as the creative force for good and knew that he was the channel through which God's good was expressed. When he prayed, his sole intention was to know union with the force of life, and we can see by his life that he achieved it.

Prayer is the method by which we, too, discover the presence of God within us. It is the way we prepare ourselves to hear divine inspiration. God continually pours divine ideas into our minds. Yes, we live in a fragile world, but included in this design is the constant flow of inspiration to show us how we can evolve and make things better. When we pray in the manner taught by Jesus, we improve our ability to hear divine inspiration and to act on the guidance we receive. As a result our own lives are enriched, and we in turn enhance the lives of others.

So when we are faced with an event like a devastating tornado, instead of seeing it as God's way of making us suffer, we learn to turn our minds inward to the presence of God so that we can be guided in ways that will restore order and wholeness to our lives.

The Power of Prayer

Jesus poetically describes what science is now showing to be true. Prayers are thoughts, and thoughts have power. In fact, thoughts determine our world. Science is beginning to prove what Jesus and other spiritual masters have known for centuries about the effects our thoughts have on the world around us.

Physicists have shown that life is creative energy and that everything emerges from this energy field. Our outer world reflects what we hold true in thought. As we become more conscious of this connection, we become proactive co-creators rather than victims of circumstances. And prayer is the tool by which we become more deliberate in how and what we create.

Research has shown that people do better overall when they maintain a positive outlook on life. Doctors often suggest that patients use methods such as visualization when combating illnesses like cancer. We know that relaxation exercises can lower blood pressure and enhance our overall health. These are all forms of prayer and are ways that we tune in to the creative process.

∞

Dr. Larry Dossey is renowned for his work compiling research on the effects of prayer on illnesses. The physician cites several studies on his Web site that demonstrate the effects of prayer on rates of healing. One study, conducted by Dr. Elisabeth Targ at California Pacific Medical Center in San Francisco, investigated the effects of distant healing or prayer on patients with advanced AIDS. The results, according to Dossey, showed that those receiving prayer "survived in greater numbers, got sick less often, and recovered faster than those who did not receive prayer." As Dossey explained, "These are impressive double-blind studies, meaning that no one knows who is receiving prayer and who isn't."[4]

When we pray, we consciously connect to the invisible energy field of infinite possibility. When we enter prayer with clear hearts and minds, free of our own personal agendas, we surrender to the highest good for all involved. We begin to see and trust that there is a higher idea waiting to be discovered. We move beyond our small, limited perspective of the world and see ourselves as active participants in the creative process.

But prayer includes much more than just our thoughts. Our "feeling" nature is the true energy behind our prayers. When we pray, we must focus on our thoughts *and* our feelings. In *The Secrets of the Lost Mode of Prayer*, Gregg Braden told the story of a time he accompanied a Native American friend to the desert to "pray rain." His friend drew a circle on the ground, stood in the circle for a few moments in silence, then turned to Braden and said, "Let's go."

Braden's response was, "Wait a minute, I thought you were going to pray for rain." His friend replied that he did not pray *for* rain; he prayed rain. He knew rain, he felt rain. He saw the reality of rain in the field of infinite possibility, and his role was to know it with every fiber of his being in order to bring in into manifestation.[5] I believe that this is what Jesus did. As he prayed, he felt and became the quality that he desired in order to manifest it.

Relearning the Lord's Prayer

So how do we begin to pray differently? In Luke 11:1, Jesus' disciples asked the same question, and Jesus responded by gifting them with one of the most powerful models of prayer known to man: the Lord's Prayer. Many of us have been taught that it was the prayer we were supposed to memorize. But when we simply take it as one more thing that we are required to do, we miss its beauty and power. The Gospel of Matthew (6:9-14) has a more expanded version that I will use for this discussion. It is the quintessential Jesus prayer, so we should treat it as a perfect blueprint. Each line gives very specific directions as to how we should pray.

Jesus began his prayer with *"Our Father."* This is our cue to acknowledge that there is a greater power and presence at work in our lives. He had the remarkable ability to see God as absolute principle and at the same time personal. He was not put off by the impartial, universal nature of God. In fact, Jesus had implicit trust in God as principle.

Charles Fillmore, in *The Revealing Word*, describes principle as "the underlying plan by which Spirit moves in expressing itself." He goes on to say, "God immanent in the universe is the great underlying cause of all manifestation; the source from which form proceeds."[6] Jesus knew that God as principle was unchanging and not subject to the whims of humankind. He could trust that certain spiritual laws were always active, whether or not he understood and used them. He tells us in Matthew 5:45: "For he makes his sun rise on the evil and on the good, and sends the rain on the righteous and unrighteous."

At the same time, Jesus had a very warm and intimate relationship with God. Jesus saw God as a living, loving parent concerned only for her creation. Jesus never questioned his own value or wondered if he was loved. He just assumed that all of these things were true. He claimed God as his own and expected that God would respond in kind. He addressed God with terms of intimacy and adoration.

The term *Father* is one example that Jesus gave us. It is not important that we use the same name. Rather, it is Jesus' way of inviting us to see ourselves in a very close relationship with God. So begin to experiment with the different names that bring God near to you. For some it may be Father-Mother, Spirit, Divine Love, or Wisdom, Allah, Abba. The name truly does not matter. Choose one that has deep personal meaning to you and allows you to feel a connection with the Creator of your being.

Jesus then went on to place God: "*in heaven.*" When Jesus spoke of the kingdom of heaven, he was not speaking of a geographical place; rather, he was referring to a place of consciousness. When we live from the kingdom-of-heaven consciousness, we are keenly aware of God and God's good in our lives. We are cognizant of the creative force moving in, through and all around us, and we see our part in bringing the force of God alive. With a flash of divine insight, we understand that the kingdom of heaven is at hand. It is here now, waiting to be discovered and experienced.

Jesus continues with "*hallowed be your name,*" telling us that God's name, God's essence, is sacred. When we say God's name, whatever that name may be for us, we say it with reverence for the vastness of God. We stand before the mystery of the Divine, reassured, according to Muller in *Learning to Pray*, "that the essential nature of God is always present and available to us."[7]

Jesus said, "*Your will be done on earth as it is in heaven.*" One of the most powerful prayers we can utter is "Your will be done." In those four simple words, we claim the infinite presence of God in our lives. We understand that God's desire is that we be happy. She wills wholeness, abundance and beauty.

Remember, Jesus said that he came so that we might have life and have it abundantly. When we live from the kingdom-of-heaven consciousness, this is fact for us. We may not see it immediately in our outer world. But as it is in consciousness, so it becomes in the physical realm. That is another way of saying "As it is in heaven, so it is on earth."

"Give us this day our daily bread." This can be restated as "God, you are giving this day to us, you are supplying us with the bread and substance that we need in order to live the life of glory that you have designed for us." God gives us the day, and God gives us the means to live this day with joy and fulfillment. Jesus not only believed this principle, he also demonstrated it in everything he did.

It bears repeating that Jesus knew that when he was created in the mind of God, he was given all he needed to live life fully. What kind of father would not provide for his children? Today we arrest such parents and charge them with child abuse and neglect. In Matthew 7:9, 11, Jesus told his listeners, "Is there anyone among you who, if your child asks for bread, will give a stone .... If you then, who are evil, know how to give good gifts to your children, how much will your Father in heaven give good things to those who ask him." This was Jesus' truth.

We can look at nature to confirm that truth. Jesus told us to notice the birds in the air and to see how they are fed even though they do not toil. Nature tends toward growth and expansion. Under healthy circumstances, all forms of life are given what they need to live and thrive in their environment. That is the natural order of things.

"And forgive us our debts, as we also have forgiven our debtors."
This line reflects classic cause and effect. God does not forgive
us because God never condemns us. God sees only our perfection. God created us with the continual urge to evolve. We
have an incredible capacity for acts of good. By the same
token, we have the capacity for unthinkable acts of evil. But
dark acts are simply a result of people forgetting who they are
as divine beings. So we ask for forgiveness. Again, we ask not
because we need God to forgive but because forgiveness
changes the way we see ourselves and those around us. We
will study forgiveness as a separate spiritual practice in the
next chapter.

Aramaic-Bible translator George Lamsa presents the next
line as, *"Do not let us enter into temptation but deliver us from
evil."* When Jesus used the word *evil*, he was acknowledging
that in our humanness, we are capable of horribly inhumane
acts toward one another.

With this line, we are asking to be delivered from our own
dark tendencies that surface when we feel alone and afraid.
As we are delivered from the potential for evil acts that exists
within ourselves, we are better able to extend compassion
and generosity. As a result, we grow these qualities in ourselves and in our world.

Many teachers have suggested that the entire prayer was
actually meant to be an affirmation. So it would read something like this:

Our Father, which is in heaven, holy is your name, my name. Your kingdom is come, your will is done, here in the physical plain as it is ordained in the realm invisible. You give us this day and our daily bread. Our trespasses are forgiven as we forgive others for perceived transgressions. You leave us not in temptation but rather you deliver us from evil. Amen (or "So it is").

As Jesus internalized this prayer and made it his reality, he discovered the nature of his being as one with his Creator. He awoke to his true spiritual nature and had the audacity to make bold statements such as "I am the way, and the truth, and the life. No one comes to the Father except through me. If you know me, you will know my Father also. From now on you do know him and have seen him" (John 14:6-7).

Those are powerful words, and you can see why some people thought that Jesus was committing blasphemy. But to Jesus it would have been blasphemous to speak any other way. As he spent time in quiet communion with his Creator, he saw himself as God saw him—unlimited, sacred and the means through which God expresses itself.

Jesus wanted us to claim these statements as our own. He told us that we are also the light of the world and not to hide our light under a bushel. When we know God as he knew God and see ourselves as Jesus did, we will let our light shine in ways that will have an impact on so many of those around us.

So as we continue to follow in Jesus' footsteps in order to replicate and surpass what he did, we take the time to enrich our prayer life in order to know God with the same intimacy and adoration that Jesus did. We understand that prayer is vital to our spiritual journey and is as necessary to the process as breathing is to living. So we begin.

Practicing the Practice

I invite you to take time with each exercise in order to deepen your own prayer life. Know that just as Jesus unlocked the power of Spirit within him, so, too, can you.

1. Begin to do some work on your image of God. Take time to write your personal history of God. Describe how you have perceived God in the past. Who or what was God, and what did your prayers sound like? Have they changed over the years? How? Then listen carefully to your prayers today for clues on how you currently see God. Do you pray hoping to convince someone of something? Do you pray with fear? All of these activities will help you see just what you do believe about God and how you interact with God.

2. Once you have developed your current picture of God, it is time to create the God you want. I have often suggested to people in my ministry that they write down the kind of God they wish for. Describe the experience you want with God, and from there an image of God will emerge.

∞

I remember when I started on this spiritual path, I saw God as a washing machine. I was releasing so much emotional baggage and so many old beliefs. I saw God as energy cleansing me in order to make room for God's greater design for me. My image of God has changed over time and continues to evolve as I continue to grow spiritually.

You have free rein. There is no "God police force" telling you that you have to believe a certain way. What image of God would instill in you a sense of faith, love and support? Write it down; play with it. Experiment. Find a name for God that feeds and nurtures you. The sky is the limit, figuratively and literally.

3. The next step is to set aside time each day to commune with God if you do not already have a dedicated prayer time. Bring your new image of God along with you into this time. Jesus told us to go within to the secret closet. The best way to learn God is to do God. We do that by consciously spending time becoming more aware of God. There are a plethora of books and tapes out there describing ways to pray and meditate. See some in the Endnotes at the end of this book.

4. Find a phrase or affirmation that you can use as your mantra. Jesus gave us a number of affirmative statements that he knew were true about himself. During your prayer and meditation time, repeat one of these statements aloud. You might choose to use Jesus' powerful statement, "I am

the way, the truth and the light." Say it slowly to yourself. Allow your entire being to hear the words. Let them filter down to your heart center. Begin to ask: *What does it mean to be the way, the truth and the light? Can I see myself in that way? Am I shining my light in what I do and say? Have I been a light for people to follow?* Take his statement and make it your own. You can do this same process with any powerful word or phrase that strikes a chord with you.

5. You may decide that journaling is an effective way of praying. This is the form that prayer often takes for me. I spend my prayer time journaling or writing letters to God or Spirit or Infinite Wisdom or whatever I am calling God at that time. I write my thoughts and feelings, prayers and wishes. I allow my higher self to take the pen and write to me and through me. I don't worry about grammar, spelling or punctuation. I simply let the thoughts and feelings flow. It is amazing what gets revealed during this process and to realize that deep down, within the marrow of our being, we already know what we need to know.

6. Use the Lord's Prayer as a model during your prayer time. Focus on each line of the prayer and contemplate what it means to you. What is your name for God? What do you see as God's will for you? Can you see how God provides you with your daily spiritual and physical nourishment? Rewrite the prayer in your own words and use it during your prayer time.

∞

These are just a few suggestions to help you get started if you do not already have a daily practice. The point is to begin. You initiate the intention to see and know God. It is a time to be filled up, nourished and inspired by—and infused with—life. It will be the most important time you spend during the day, and it will be the greatest gift you give yourself. So begin today. Begin to spend time knowing God, and see how you begin to model and replicate what our master teacher, Jesus, did.

Forgiveness

Forgiveness is the fourth spiritual practice, and it is central to Jesus' teachings. It is the most powerful method available to us for cultivating a kinder, more loving world. Jesus' whole ministry evolved around the two commandments of loving God and loving our neighbor as ourselves.

Everything Jesus taught and modeled for us was intended to show us how to love one another and the power in that simple act. But Jesus also knew that as human beings, we struggle with feelings of betrayal, hurt and anger. When we're feeling those emotions, it becomes almost impossible for us even to be around the perpetrators, much less love them.

Forgiveness was not a new idea for Jesus' listeners. The principle of pardoning those who have harmed another is woven throughout the Old Testament. But Jesus knew that those parts were often ignored, and people latched onto the text that accommodated their need for revenge.

Exodus gives a number of different instructions on how to handle transgressions. In particular, 21:23-25 describes how, in response to serious personal injury, "you shall give life for life, eye for eye, tooth for tooth, hand for hand, foot for foot, burn for burn, wound for wound, stripe for stripe."

We can see how the need for revenge continues to be the norm today. Our entire criminal justice system is based on the idea that people need to be punished for their crimes. We believe that the victim will be vindicated if the criminal is made to suffer as the victim suffered.

Please hear me—I am not saying that we should not hold people accountable for their crimes. But until we realize that causing another person to suffer does not ultimately relieve our suffering, we will be as imprisoned as the one who committed the actual crime. We are victims of our own system.

Revenge Is Not Sweet

The lesson that Jesus' listeners heard 2,000 years ago was as radical then as it is now. In Matthew 5:38-39, Jesus addresses several aspects of forgiveness. He says, "You have heard that it was said, 'Eye for eye, and tooth for tooth.' But I tell you, do not resist an evildoer. If someone strikes you on the right cheek, turn the other also."

How often have you heard people say that this teaching is just not realistic, that you can't go around letting other people walk all over you? But Jesus was very clear about this point. Revenge had to be eliminated and replaced by something almost inconceivable.

He also stated in Matthew 5:42-44, "You have heard that it was said, 'You shall love your neighbor and hate your enemy.' But I say to you: Love your enemies and pray for those who persecute you." The people hearing Jesus' words at the time understood the importance of loving their neighbors, but Jesus, the master psychologist, knew that any time we are angry at other people—whether or not they are someone we love—they become our enemy. They are against us, and therefore we make them wrong and, ultimately, our foes. Jesus knew that he had to teach this lesson in such a way that there was no loophole.

Even today, loving one's enemy is an idea that seems to go against sound judgment. Doing this means putting ourselves at the mercy of another and just invites more of the same. Or so we think.

Revenge is actually part of our brain chemistry. During a piece the *CBS Sunday Morning* news show aired in April 2009 on forgiveness, reporter Martha Teichner interviewed a psychology professor who said that revenge is like an instinct. "The brain system that produces revenge is the same system we use when we're looking for something to eat when we are hungry. Desire: It's the desire to satisfy a craving."

On the other hand, he explained, "There is a natural, evolved capacity to forgive that also exists in every human mind on the planet." He went on to explain that revenge can be like junk food: It might make us feel better in the short run, but forgiveness is better for our overall good health.[1]

Bruce Lipton, a former medical school professor, researcher and author of *The Biology of Belief*, gives a beautiful explanation of how our physiological response changes when we experience stress. When life is flowing along and all is well, the body's energies are directed toward maintaining life-sustaining functions such as digestion, respiration and circulation. The body is able to focus on the natural process of renewing and restoring its parts. The immune system does its job by combating any invaders we come in contact with during our day. The body works as it is designed to, providing us with the energy and focus we need to be fully present.

But when we feel stressed or threatened, as is the case when we nurse a hurt or resentment, the body goes into a fight-or-flight mode. As a result, all the energy that goes toward functioning normally is now redirected into those systems that are geared toward protection. And unlike during a normal fight-or-flight response, we don't give our bodies a chance to recover when we continue to nurse old wounds. Lipton compares the effect of prolonged stress on the body to a runner being in a perpetual state of "get set" on the runner's blocks. The runner's body is poised and ready to run, muscles tight and mind focused, but he or she never gets the "go" gun.[2]

Resentment actually makes us dumber. All of this stress adds up, reducing our ability to think clearly, compromising the efficiency of our immune system and impairing our ability to digest food properly. Blood is diverted from the stomach and intestine to outer limbs in order to prepare them to run if we need to. The blood flow to the forebrain, where we process complex information, is redirected to the hindbrain, the center of our reflexes.

That same story on *CBS Sunday Morning* featured two people who had both lost sons to a drunk driver late one night. The father of one son stated that if he forgives, then his son's death is for nothing. It was as if his life had frozen in time and he was unable to move beyond the loss and anger. In contrast, the other boy's mother said that she could not live with hate and bitterness in her heart. Not only did she forgive, but she took it a step further and decided to work with the young man who had caused the accident by going to schools with him to lecture on the dangers of drinking and driving.

She was able to channel her loss into something positive by educating people about the dangers of drunk driving. Imagine the impact she makes when she steps out on stage with the young man who took her son's life! Her forgiveness has allowed her to use the situation to make a contribution to her world. She is not frozen but is expanding, and as a result is also expanding the understanding of those around her.[3]

Why Forgiveness?

In order for us to move past the idea that we must make someone pay for his or her sins against us, Jesus taught a very different kind of lesson—he taught the power of forgiveness. He knew that in order for us to experience the kind of life he saw for us, we had to learn to let go of the hurt and anger that blocked our good from us. We had to learn how to forgive. Only then could the kingdom of heaven become a reality.

Forgiveness liberates us. It frees us from the limiting stories of our past. We don't feel so alone, and the world becomes less scary. Consequently, we become less defensive and more open to life. When we forgive, we are able to see the world the way we were meant to see it, as having beauty and grace.

So what exactly does Jesus mean when he tells us to forgive? As with the other practices, he presents a very different view of forgiveness from the one most of us have been taught. I know I used to think forgiveness was something I granted other people when they did something "to me," seeing myself as a victim and others as the villains. I would force myself to forgive because I thought it was the right thing to do, but in reality I had no concept of what it truly meant to forgive. I said I forgave someone, and yet the peace and well-being that Jesus promised eluded me.

As I have continued along my own spiritual path, forgiveness has come to mean something very different. No longer is it something that I grant another; it is the practice that allows me to shift the way I see myself, the event and the other person or persons involved.

Part of the difficulty that many of us have with forgiveness is that we see other people as one-dimensional; we characterize others according to a single hurtful impression or incident. This image becomes frozen in our minds and colors the way we see them from that time forward, regardless of what they do or who they are. As a result, we impose a barrier between ourselves and them.

Feeling wounded and bruised, we then generalize our experience and become guarded in all of our relationships. We become afraid to make ourselves vulnerable. But without vulnerability, we are incapable of knowing joy and living spontaneously.

As we mature spiritually and incorporate true forgiveness into our daily routines, we learn to transcend our hurt and offer compassion and understanding instead. We begin to see that the world is not black and white, and none of us is all "good" or all "bad." No longer do harmful acts come only from "those people."

In forgiving others, we are neither excusing inexcusable behavior nor letting anyone off the hook. Rather, we are acknowledging that we are all capable of heinous acts, along with acts of incredible kindness and compassion, given the right circumstances. Practicing forgiveness fosters our ability to recognize that our humanity and divinity coexist.

So how do we know if we need to forgive? Any time we judge or blame or feel victimized or put out or put upon or feel the need to protect or defend ourselves, we need to forgive. All of those feelings are indications that we have taken personally something that someone else did.

Feeling anger, guilt, fear or shame is also an indication that we have some forgiveness work to do. Such emotions indicate that we have mistakenly put someone else in the position of making us feel happy, safe and valued. We have turned our power over to that person in the belief that he or she is supposed to provide whatever it is we think we need.

When we place unreasonable expectations on others, wanting them to give us our sense of value and well-being, we become hurt and disappointed because people inevitably let us down. The problem is that we have looked outside ourselves for our nourishment instead of tapping into the source within.

We go on to create beliefs about the world based on these experiences. We say that it is an unfriendly place and we can't depend on people. We believe that if we make ourselves vulnerable, we are setting ourselves up to be hurt. We think the world is unjust and feel the need to fight for what is ours.

What Did Jesus Do?

We find a clear example of this predicament in the parable of the vineyard workers in Matthew 20:1-16. The owner of the vineyard went out to hire workers at nine in the morning, at noon and then again around four in the afternoon. When it came time to pay the workers, the owner paid everyone equally regardless of the amount of work they did. The workers who started at nine and at noon were outraged that the workers who were only there for an hour received the same compensation that they did.

Illustrated here is the old idea of forgiveness, which is that people earn it only if they prove themselves worthy. It is assumed that we will identify only with the workers who came earlier in the day. Jesus was suggesting, however, that we have all been the 9 a.m. workers and the 4 p.m. workers. We deserve love and acceptance regardless of whether we show up in the morning or in the afternoon. The parable shatters the idea of forgiveness or love as something we earn. It is there simply because we are here. It is a lesson in grace.

When we are focused on things being fair and what others are getting or what we're not, it becomes impossible for us to offer to others the kind of compassion and spaciousness of Spirit that Jesus teaches. Our fears and narrow view of the world block the power of God from being expressed through us. We are no longer willing to be open to others, a key ingredient in Jesus' model.

When we forgive, however, we release the blockage and give Spirit a clear channel for expression in our world. We once again become the conduit through which love and graciousness are manifested. We begin to see our own inherent goodness and grace as well as that of others. We realize that others are not the source of our happiness; our happiness is generated from within. We recognize that no one can diminish us unless we give that person the power to do so.

Remember that the world around us responds according to how we view it. If we see the world as a hurtful and dangerous place, then that will continue to be our experience. If we see ourselves as unworthy, then we will attract people who reinforce that self-image. We will also interpret the actions of other people through that broken lens—regardless of what they do or don't do—because we are incapable of recognizing and accepting love. And on and on it goes.

Forgiveness breaks the cycle. With forgiveness come new belief patterns, and as a result, our lives change. We become better able to see God in all situations, in all people and, most important, in ourselves. Forgiveness also encourages us to see that it takes two to tango, and we begin to accept that we had a part in the dance. It's an acknowledgment that we are capable of the same acts that we feel have been done to us.

Jesus portrayed this beautifully in John with the story of the adulterous woman. He came upon a crowd who had condemned a woman for committing adultery. Jewish law said that she should be stoned, and the Jewish leaders who were present asked Jesus what he thought should be done with her. He bent down and wrote in the sand. Then, with pure eloquence, he said, "Let anyone among you who is without sin be the first to throw a stone at her" (John 8:7). They all walked away because they knew that none of them was without sin.

In one way or another, we have all fallen short of the perfect image that God has for us. Forgiveness helps us remember that we are all broken in some way and do hurtful things in our brokenness. All hurtful acts originate from the same illusion that we are separate beings who are meant to survive on our own. Forgiveness puts us in touch with the pain that comes from that sense of separation and helps cultivate understanding and acceptance.

Forgiveness means seeing things differently. It means reframing our hurtful experiences, seeing ourselves whole even amid painful circumstances. Then we become willing to see how we may be perpetuating damaging patterns of behavior. We can begin to take responsibility for our less-than-loving actions from this point on, and with self-awareness and compassion see how we, too, have contributed to these situations. We are no longer completely the victim or the perpetrator.

I believe that Jesus gave us the ultimate lesson in forgiveness during the final days of his life. He was beaten, ridiculed and finally put to death. Through it all, he stayed centered and composed, maintaining his dignity and his compassion. Even in the face of extreme circumstances, he stayed true to his teachings.

We, on the other hand, are more apt to condemn one another because we want to see others hurt. The problem is that this approach does not give us the desired results. Peace simply does not come at someone else's expense. We cannot pass judgment on another person without condemning our-selves. Jesus knew this when he said, "Forgive us our debts, as we also have forgiven our debtors" (Matthew 6:12). It is only when we let go of judgment and condemnation that we are free from their effects. Truly, what goes around comes around.

Life Journeys

On October 2, 2006, the Amish community in Lancaster, Pennsylvania, gave the world a powerful lesson in forgive-ness. According to news reports, Charles Carl Roberts, a truck driver who picked up milk from area Amish farms, entered one of their schools and began shooting, killing five of their daughters. It was an unthinkable crime against a community that stood for peace. In the aftermath, instead of demanding justice and revenge, however, the Amish sought out Roberts' family and offered comfort and support. It was reported that one of the Amish men held the shooter's sobbing father in his arms. They prayed for the family, themselves and the world, asking for peace and forgiveness.[4]

Roberts' family was profoundly moved by this display of compassion. Instead of anger and bitterness, blame and vic-timization, the members of this community were able to use the wounds in their hearts to bring about deep healing.

The Amish, in seeking to follow the model of their teacher Jesus, are a culture rooted in forgiveness. It is not just a vague abstraction for them; forgiveness is an act as well as a guide for responding to challenges. Imagine what the world would be like if we were all able to offer forgiveness, deep compassion and love in the face of that kind of violation! Violence would stop in its tracks.

Forgiveness was one of Jesus' last acts on the cross when he said "Father, forgive them, for they do not know what they are doing" (Luke 23:24). Even then he demonstrated truth. He knew that the people who were condemning and crucifying him really did not know what they were doing. Their actions were based on their understanding of the world.

Rev. Gary Simmons, author of *The I of the Storm*, explains that when we feel hurt by someone else's actions, it is because we mistakenly believe that there is something defective or missing in us—otherwise we would not be affected by what that person had done. So when we forgive, we reclaim those supposedly inadequate aspects of ourselves. We reframe the experience in a way that allows us to see ourselves as we were created: whole and complete.[5]

At this point, we can also ask how we might have responded differently in the past if we had recognized that we were worthy, valued, confident, strong and wise. Once we have those answers, we see that it really is not about the other person; it is about how we perceive the situation and ourselves. We realize that we have 100 percent choice in what we believe and, consequently, how we behave. We discover that there never really is anything to forgive. We all act from our own woundedness, and if we could do better, we would.

Forgiveness gives us the tools to respond with love and understanding, and doing so gives us the power to radically shift the dynamics of any situation. The Amish community in Lancaster has shown us that.

A friend once shared with me her experience of being raped. She told me that somehow she was able to transcend her rage and terror during the experience to see her attacker as someone who was crying out for love. She felt those emotions evaporate and instead offered acceptance. Afterward, she said, she also did not have the expected feelings of fear and shame.

This is not to say that she did not report the crime to the justice system and cooperate so that the man would experience the consequences of his actions. But during that situation, she saw how she had the choice of allowing this man to rob her of her dignity. She chose to see both her and her attacker as originating from the substance of God, which allowed her to see his divine essence even in the face of such a horrendous act. I cannot say that I would have the same ability to stay centered. But when I heard her story, I realized that I do always have the choice. Forgiveness gives me the tools enabling me to choose dignity and grace over anger and separation.

There is a line in *A Course in Miracles* by Dr. Helen Schucman that says, "God does not forgive, because God never condemns."[6] Universal Power and Presence cannot be offended. Creative energy sees only beauty and perfection.

God acknowledges that we are on a journey and move forward continuously, regardless of how shaky that journey is at times. This is how God created us. At the same time, God wants only good for us. Both of these truths make it impossible for God to condemn us.

So how, then, do we forgive? Where do we even start? First, enlist help. We are wired for community. Find a friend or therapist who will support what you are attempting to do. Ideally, the person you select should be someone who has gone through the process and is committed to the spiritual practice of forgiveness.

We need to be honest about the effect that certain events and people have on us. Many of us, especially those on a spiritual path, tend to minimize that impact. We think we are supposed to be above feeling hurt. If we do have "negative" feelings, it means that we are not spiritual enough. I believe that we can reach a point where we are hardly affected by the behavior of others, but first we must deal with our emotional baggage.

When my mother was being treated for addiction, I learned for the first time that she acted the way she did when I was growing up because she had the disease of alcoholism. I felt relief the first time I heard this explanation, but at the same time, I felt as if I had been stripped of permission to be angry or hurt.

I thought I had forgiven my mother, and had even convinced myself that I didn't have anything to forgive her for because she was incapable of making any other choices. I wanted to be in that place of forgiveness, and I was there intellectually. I spent two years denying and stuffing my feelings. But when the anger and resentment began to manifest as chronic illness and depression, I realized that I had to face them. My unattended pain was still coloring my perception of her and of myself. I realized that I could not truly forgive until I had walked through the hurt that was lodged in my heart.

I learned to separate my mother's behaviors from the reality of who she was. Because I had committed myself to forgiveness and had begun to understand its nature, I was able to go through the healing process without cutting myself off from her. That did not mean my buttons were not pushed by her. In fact, I was extremely sensitive to her behavior, but I had a process that enabled me to deal with it.

Healing happens in layers. So as you incorporate a forgiveness practice into your daily spiritual discipline, be aware that even if you have already gone through this process in relation to a specific person or event, the issue may come up again. But that does not mean you went through the process incorrectly. It simply means that you have the opportunity to heal deeper and to learn more profoundly what Jesus taught us about love and goodness.

When we forgive someone, we change our patterns so that we are less likely to continue destructive behaviors. If we blame the other person, then we are doomed to repeat the pattern. If you have ever noticed that you deal with the same scenario over and over again—same story, different players—then there is something about it that you need to forgive and release. Once you see how you have contributed to a situation, you are no longer at the other person's mercy. You can make different choices, and thus change your experience.

In Matthew 18:21, Peter asked Jesus, "How often should I forgive? As many as seven times?" Jesus replied in verse 22, "Not seven times, but, I tell you, seventy-seven times," which means that we never stop forgiving. As long as we continue to exist in this physical form and see ourselves as separate from one another, we will have forgiveness work to do.

So I invite you into the sacred process of forgiveness. The process I have included here has worked well for me over the years. Join me so that together we can experience the freedom and heaven that Jesus promised.

Practicing the Practice

1. Start by identifying the people in your life whom you need to forgive. Sit down with a pad of paper and an inventory of those people. Start with the major players. Bring each one to mind and ask, *Do I feel hurt or disappointed when I think of this person? Is there something I need to forgive him or her for?* If you feel any tightness in your body, then you need to forgive this person for something. If you have any unloving judgment about this individual, then you need to forgive.

2. Once you have your list, you can then begin the process of forgiveness. There are numerous ways to forgive. One of the most powerful ways that I have found is to write letters. I take time, remove myself from life's distractions and write letters to the people I believe have hurt me. I write down all of the things that I would like to say in person but I know are not appropriate. I basically let them have it on paper. I write about all of the evil things I believe they did to me, and I write about how I have been affected.

These letters often have the tone of a victim. And that is okay at this stage of the game. I need to be able to see myself as a victim for a while, especially if I have pretended that everything is rosy. This is an opportunity to let my feelings of hurt, abandonment and betrayal rip. I write and write and write until there is nothing left to write.

3. Next, I encourage you to read your letters to someone else. Don't mail the letters to the actual people they're directed to (this is your work, not theirs). But it is important that someone else hear you and witness your pain, that you let another person validate your experience and give you the comfort you may never have received. This is not a time for you and your witness to bash the person you are forgiving. It is a time to have someone hear your hurt so that you can let it go. Bring plenty of tissues, and have a few pillows around in case you need to pound them.

4. Once you have finished this process, take some time alone, and ask if there is anything you have missed. You have an

empty space now that was once filled with anger, blame and fear. Allow the presence of the Holy Spirit to fill you. Take some time and see your inner light grow and expand as it has been set free.

5. World-renowned author and speaker Louise Hay offers a powerful meditation in her book *You Can Heal Your Life* that is a great way to complete the process: Envision yourself and the person you are forgiving as young children. See how both of you are in pain and in need of comfort. Imagine yourself taking both children into your arms and giving them the comfort and love they are longing for. Imagine yourself as an adult placing these precious children—these images of yourself and the person you are forgiving—into your heart space. Then promise to love both you and the person you are forgiving and to see both of you as the children of God that you are. When you can imagine someone as a little girl or boy, it is hard to stay angry and hurt.[7]

6. Make forgiveness a daily discipline. Gary Simmons outlines a reconciliation process in his book *The I of the Storm*. He suggests that each evening we ask, *Am I harboring any hurt or resentment? Have I allowed the behavior of another to cause me to feel diminished in any way?* Once we have recognized those times when we felt diminished, we can go back and replay the situations in our minds, seeing ourselves the way God sees us: as whole, loving, capable.

Then we can see how we respond differently when we know these things about ourselves.

Continuing the process, we go on to ask these questions: *Have I done anything to harm or diminish another? Is there something I need to ask forgiveness for?* We make it a point not to delay but to seek out and reconcile with that person the next day.[8]

When we do this, we stay connected to Source. We stay connected to one another; we stay connected to the creative life force. We see how our experience is directly influenced by how we see things.

So as we continue our journey toward emulating what Jesus taught and modeled, we incorporate the practice of forgiveness. We practice seeing people and ourselves as God sees us on a daily basis. As a result, we become a clear conduit for all the attributes of God. We experience what Jesus taught and promised.

-6-

Gratitude

Gratitude, the next spiritual practice in our series of nine, is a powerful tool that improves our ability to follow Jesus' example. Each time we practice it, we become a bit more aware of the reality of God all around us. Something in us changes, making us happier, more productive people. Ultimately, it is a foolproof way to help us awaken spiritually. Jesus was a master at the art of gratitude, and he included it in every demonstration he gave.

The New Testament reports how Jesus consistently and publicly expressed gratitude when teaching and ministering to others. He gave thanks before each miracle, and he prayed aloud to make sure that those around him knew how important it was. In fact, when he raised Lazarus from the dead, he told onlookers that he gave thanks not for God's sake but for the sake of those who were watching.

Why did he do this? God certainly didn't need the gratitude. And seeing God as an entity that insists we express gratitude before it fulfills our desires would mean reducing

111

God to a mean-spirited egomaniac. Instead, Jesus was showing us how gratitude is a tool that prepares us to receive God's goodness. It prepares our hearts and minds to receive the abundance that is already ours. Giving thanks in advance primes us to receive what we desire, a desire that is already fulfilled in the invisible realm. It enables us to cultivate enough belief to make the seemingly impossible possible.

We all know that gratitude is important. It is the custom of civilized people to say "thank you" after receiving something. And most of the time, it is a great feeling to be on the receiving end of a gift or an acknowledgment. Often we have difficulty accepting someone else's generosity, and I will address that later in this chapter. For now it is safe to say that most of us are grateful when we are blessed in some way, but gratitude continues to be predicated on getting something. It is still the effect. We wait until we think there is something to be grateful for before expressing our gratitude.

Jesus saw it differently. He saw gratitude not as the effect but as the cause. If we examine many of his public miracles, we see him purposely giving thanks in advance.

Gratitude in Action

The story of how Jesus fed the five thousand is a wonderful illustration of the practice of gratitude as a causative agent. You'll recall from your Bible studies that Jesus had been teaching all day to a crowd of thousands of men, women and children on a hillside. Evening came, and the people were hungry. Dealing with 5,000 or so restless, hungry people in the middle of the desert would certainly have been a challenge. Jesus' disciples knew this and started to get a bit nervous; in fact, they tried to whisk Jesus out of there before the crowd became too disorderly. I see them as first-century secret service ready to put Jesus into a chariot and get him out of there fast.

But Jesus would not have any of that. First he suggested to the disciples that they feed everyone. They reacted with a doubter's typical response: "How do you expect us to take care of all of these people? What could you possibly be thinking?" You can almost hear them mumbling among themselves about how Jesus had been in the sun too long and must be suffering from heat stroke.

Jesus then took the matter into his own hands and asked those around him to gather any food they could find among the crowd. There was a young boy in the crowd who had two loaves of bread and five fish to share. Making no judgment, Jesus acknowledged what he had, and with poise and confidence, he took the bread and fish and blessed them.

To the people watching, that might have seemed a bit odd. Why would the master bless this measly amount of fish and bread when he knew that it was not even a decent start to feeding all of these people?

But this is why Jesus is the master and we are the students. He did not necessarily see the fish and bread as enough. In fact, as an intelligent man, he knew that in its present form, that food was not going to satisfy everyone's hunger. But instead of seeing what he did not have, he focused on what he had. He focused on the fish and loaves as evidence of the substance of God, and knew that there was more where that came from. And so he gave thanks in advance by blessing the food, trusting that the crowd's need would be met.

According to *Merriam-Webster's Collegiate Dictionary*, to bless means "to confer prosperity or happiness upon." When Jesus blessed the fish and loaves, he saw the appearance of prosperity and gave thanks for it. His gratitude gave him the ability to look beyond the appearance of insufficiency and instead see the potential waiting in the invisible realm.

Unlike Jesus, we get locked into appearances. We perceive things with our senses and form opinions that create our beliefs, and then claim that what we see is the gospel truth. Jesus taught us to look beyond what our five senses tell us to the realm of Spirit, or the invisible, and to give thanks for what we know is present even though we might not be able to see it. Blessing something with the power to confer goodness is another way of saying "thank you" in advance.

Charles Fillmore, co-founder of Unity, wrote in his book *Prosperity* that scientists were close to discovering how to manifest items from the ether.[1] Is it possible that one day we may be able to literally pull a loaf of bread out of thin air? Who knows? But it may have been what happened on that hillside thousands of years ago.

Later in that book, Fillmore shared how God is the substance from which everything is created. God is not the man in the sky who drops food at our doorstep; rather, God fills us with divine ideas and guidance that, when followed, result in the outer satisfaction of our needs and desires. Whether we pull what we need from thin air or heed the direction from divine inspiration, gratitude is an important ingredient in unlocking the divine power and presence of Spirit.

However it happened that day on the hillside, Jesus fed thousands of people—either with actual food, by his words or both—and as a result, his listeners were changed by the event. They became more aware of God's good in their lives. Something life-transforming happened that day, and its effects continue to reverberate. And giving thanks in advance was a vital part of the day's lesson.

We in the modern world say "thank you" in advance all the time. Think of the times you have ordered something over the phone. You described the item and even provided your credit card information, trusting that within a given amount of time, the mail carrier would drop off the item at your house. You then thanked the salesperson for his or her service and the item.

Expressing thanks in advance with God is no different. We're acknowledging a need and giving thanks before actually having it met. As Jesus showed us, in order for our thanks to be effective, we must ask from a state of trust or belief that our requests will be fulfilled.

The words "thank you" by themselves have their own life-transforming energy. There was a television commercial a while back showing people making insensitive comments. One woman walked up to another in a grocery store and asked with excitement when she was due. The overweight woman looked at her with dismay and said, "I'm not pregnant!" The first woman then began simply to say "thank you," until she was back in the woman's good graces. She used her thank-you's as a causative agent to change the situation. Their interaction wonderfully illustrates how the phrase alone carries enough power to change the dynamics of a situation.

Practicing gratitude, or appreciation, is powerful. When we're doing it, it is hard—impossible, in fact—to stay focused on what we think is missing. In Chapter 3, on faith, I wrote about how we magnify and multiply what we focus upon. When we live in a state of gratitude, our focus shifts to the good in our lives, on what is working.

This does not mean that we are in denial. We are not ignoring the facts in our lives. But Jesus modeled faith that God, or Infinite Substance, is always present and active, even when that presence is not obvious. He understood that he was the channel through which this energy expressed itself. He built his life around this belief, and it showed.

Again, he knew that the food he had before him was not enough, but he focused on the unlimited supply of substance, and God as the infinite supplier of good. Jesus saw how substance flowed through him because he was a channel for God's abundance. He didn't see God as a withholder of good. He understood that even in physical form, he was not separate from the Father.

The Physics of Prayer

Science is discovering some ideas that ground this spiritual principle in the concrete world. Gregg Braden, in his book *The Isaiah Effect*, does a brilliant job explaining the quantum physics of prayer. He describes how physicists have shown that there are a multitude of possibilities available to us at any given moment. All options are there at once, waiting for us to decide where we will put our focus, which then determines which possibility will manifest.[2]

The old adage of A + B = C does not apply anymore. It is more like A + B = C, D or E or XYZ. Gratitude opens us to the possibility that anything can happen. It increases our capacity to entertain other options even if we can't begin to see how they might happen. It gives us a renewed sense of hope and brings our focus back to the possibility that things will turn out well.

As we focus on what is good in our lives, we bring the favorable possibility out from the shadows into the light of day. We clothe the desired choice and make it real with our thoughts and feelings. As we focus on gratitude, or appreciation, we give God the space to bring about other possibilities that are beyond our human understanding or imaginings.

Braden also explains the quantum theory of quanta, or bursts of light. He tells us that "the science of quantum physics has demonstrated that our world actually occurs in very short, rapid bursts of light." Each burst is one in a series of individual events "that happen very fast and very close together. Similar to the many still images that make up a moving film, these events are actually tiny pulses of light called quanta." In other words, physicists no longer see events as one fluid movement. They have discovered that circumstances are made of several isolated episodes that meld together to give the appearance of seamlessness. These separate events happen in those bursts of light.[3]

Why does this matter? The implications are huge. Just as a film editor can go through and cut out, rearrange or add frames, so can we. We no longer have to function under the illusion that we are victims of fate or that a course of action cannot be altered. We can change it at any stage simply by adjusting our frame of reference, our beliefs and our focus.

Braden explains that the moments in time where the course of an event can be altered are called choice points. He tells us, "A choice point is like a bridge making it possible to begin one path and change course to experience the outcome of a new path." He goes on to say that by moving through a choice point, we can alter a path and an outcome by changing our belief about a situation.[4]

Braden gives an example of how a patient was healed of a tumor when her practitioners "assumed the thoughts, feelings and emotion from a place where it [the tumor] never existed. The tools that make such a jump possible are found in their beliefs: the thoughts, feelings and emotions that the new reality was already in place."[5] When we operate under the assumption that all possibilities already exist at the same time, we realize that we get to choose which possibility we will experience.

Gratitude is the steering mechanism that helps us change events to something more life-affirming. We can change the direction of a particular situation, along with the outcome, by paying attention to the good and to evidence of God. Jesus did not do anything magical. He simply chose to know God at that point in time, to the exclusion of all else.

This takes us back to the discussion in Chapter 2 of clear vision which contains all the ingredients necessary to make a dream reality. As we see our mental picture, it becomes real for us—so real that we feel the emotions associated with the fulfillment of our dream before it has even occurred. If abundance for everyone is our vision, then we can feel abundant right now by focusing on what is rich in our lives. We don't have to wait for something to change in order to experience abundance.

Remember that as we focus on feelings and images that we desire, we enlarge them. By focusing on how we live in abundance in a particular moment and giving thanks for it, we expand the abundance that we desire for everyone. This is how the law works, and gratitude facilitates this process.

What Did Jesus Do?

Jesus had a vision of compassion and abundance for every man, woman and child on the planet. So when the young boy brought Jesus his fish and loaves, Jesus saw this as evidence that his vision was possible. He didn't fixate on the thousands of other people who did not have adequate food; nor did he focus on the apparent futility of it all. He concentrated on what was working in that moment as evidence of God's flow. As he focused on that and gave thanks for it, he was able to manifest it.

Our ability to express gratitude directly correlates with our ability to receive good things in our lives. Jesus mastered the art of receiving, which in turn strengthened his gratitude muscle. As simplistic as this sounds, part of developing an attitude of gratitude is expanding our ability to receive. Jesus taught us that it is okay to ask and to expect our desires to be fulfilled. He assumed that he was going to receive when he gave thanks in advance. He knew that it was necessary for him to receive in order for him to be able to give. He showed us how giving and receiving were two sides of the same coin.

So many of us were taught by very well-intentioned people that expecting to receive something was inherently wrong. The spoken or unspoken lesson was that we were not to expect much, and it was certainly not okay to ask. We were seen as greedy and unappreciative if we wanted something more or different. Many of us were also told that we must earn our good—or, to put it another way, that rewards came to those who worked hard. Consequently, many of us find it difficult to ask for what we want or need.

Once again, Jesus gave us a different example. He was very clear about this instruction: He told us to ask. He said that as we ask, we will receive. It is not because God needs us to ask. God, or Universal Substance, is there waiting for us to say yes to our abundance. We need to ask for ourselves in order to gain clarity about what it is we really want, and to prepare ourselves to receive. When we ask—truly ask—we are asking with an expectation of receiving.

Eric Butterworth, in *Spiritual Economics*, wrote, "The word *asks*, as Jesus uses it, comes from the Greek root which has a strong connotation toward 'claim or demand.'…Then why need we ask at all? It is obvious that, to God, asking was simply a claim of entitlement, a receptivity of consciousness. It is creating the condition in mind that makes the result inevitable."[6]

If we feel unworthy and don't allow ourselves to be blessed by the gifts, love and generosity of others, then how can we expect to have our desires fulfilled? We make it impossible for the universe to bring the things we desire to us. We then feel picked on and abandoned by God, which moves us farther away from a consciousness of gratitude. Ultimately, we only perpetuate the cycle of lack and unfulfilled dreams.

I love the example in the Bible in which the woman came to anoint Jesus' feet with precious oil. The apostles—Judas in particular—objected, saying that the money should be given to the poor. Jesus promptly told him that the poor would be with them always, but he would not be. He then turned his attention back to the woman who was there to minister to him and graciously received her gift. He knew that as he accepted it, the woman was blessed as well by her act of compassion and generosity.

Imagine for a moment what the world would be like if we were all givers and there were no receivers. In the relationship between the bee and the flower, nature gives us a wonderful example of this need for balance. We often think of the flower as giving the pollen to the bee, as a one-sided transaction. But as the bee goes from flower to flower, gathering the gift of pollen that each flower offers, it spreads the pollen to other flowers so that they can germinate and create new flowers. Many scientists are concerned about the recent drop in the number of bees. Without their willingness to receive the gift of the pollen from the flowers, they in turn cannot spread this gift, resulting in fewer seeds and plants.

The same goes for us. We must have people who are willing to receive our gifts. We give a gift when we are willing to take the blessing that someone is offering us without downplaying it or claiming that we don't deserve such generosity.

Part of your homework for this chapter will be to see yourself as a blessed receiver. Your challenge is to follow in the footsteps of Jesus by allowing good to flow to you and through you. You serve God and your brothers and sisters by giving God lots of room to bless and prosper you.

We have to remember that God's good does not fall from the sky. God did not literally rain manna down from heaven onto the Israelites. Rather, it is a metaphor describing how God takes care of us each step along the way. We are blessed through one another. So unless we are willing to accept others' gifts in all forms, we can't accept our good from God.

Life Journeys

What about when we find it hard to see any good? Those are the times when it is even more important to practice gratitude. Paul told us to give thanks in all things. Many of us may find this an almost impossible task. How can we give thanks when our health is failing, we have a job we despise, or our finances are in shambles? Note that he did not say to give thanks *for* all things—he said give thanks *in* all things. There is a subtle but powerful difference: He is telling us to bless the situation by realizing the power and presence of God in whatever may be going on at the time.

I once heard a story about how Myrtle Fillmore, cofounder of Unity, shared this principle with a woman who approached her for prayer, complaining that her whole body was in pain. Fillmore, after talking with her a bit, suggested that she find one part of her body that did not hurt. The woman insisted that no area was pain-free. Fillmore pressed the point until the woman finally said that the top of one of her pinkies didn't hurt.

Fillmore then gave her what probably seemed like a crazy assignment: She told the woman to bless the tip of her pinky. Every day she was to spend time blessing and appreciating her pinky, thanking it for its service and praising it. The story goes that as the woman did this, more and more of her body stopped hurting. She soon enlarged her blessing to include the other parts of her body as well, until the day came when she was pain-free.

As you read this story, what is your reaction? Do you believe it? If not, why not? Why can this not be one possibility out of millions in the incredible design of the universe? It goes back to the theory of quantum physics that says all possibilities are present in the eternal moment. We choose our possibility according to where we place our focus.

This does not mean that we pretend that everything is great when we are in pain or there is turmoil in our lives. It means that we see the presence of God amid any circumstance. We see how there is good even in what seems to be the worst situation, and how God is active. Gratitude, as Jesus demonstrated, refocuses our attention away from the perception of loss and on the possibility of good.

The *CBS Sunday Morning* news program profiled Ralph Green, a young man who had lost his leg from a gunshot wound he received while walking down the street of his Brooklyn, New York, neighborhood in the summer of 1992.

At the time, Ralph was 15 and a quarterback on the high school football team. A good student and gifted athlete, this rising star had a bright future ahead of him, giving him every reason to be angry as a victim of a random gang shooting. Instead, the program highlighted how he used his misfortune to create a whole new life that not only has made him happy but also became an inspiration to others.

Because Ralph was an "athlete at heart," the report explained how he looked for a sport that allowed him to keep competing. He found it on the ski slopes of Vail, Colorado. He now competes in the Paralympics as a skier and often speaks to high school students about the dangers of gangs. As I watched along with all the other viewers around the country, I was struck by what I saw as Ralph's ability to stay present for new and different possibilities that helped him create something good from his misfortune. This remarkable role model was seen finding things to be grateful for even in the midst of an ordeal that had the potential to destroy him, and as a result, we can see how he is a happy man contributing to the well-being of others.[7]

The story of Joseph, son of Jacob, in Genesis beautifully illustrates the power of giving thanks in all things. If you remember, his brothers sold him into slavery as a young boy. He eventually landed in Egypt and, through a series of synchronicities, found himself the most powerful man in Egypt other than the Pharaoh. One day, when all the land was facing a famine, Joseph's family, who did not recognize their brother, came to him asking for help. Joseph responded with love and generosity and told them that even though they had acted in evil when they betrayed Joseph, good came from it. The tale shows how the spirit of gratitude gives us the energy and impetus to turn difficult situations around and create something good from them.

Who has not at some point looked back to give thanks for a difficult period in life? With hindsight we could see how it was the catalyst we needed to make changes. If the event had not happened, we would have continued with the same barren pattern.

Gratitude also increases our ability to celebrate the success of others. Jealousy is a demon I have struggled with my entire life. Somewhere I developed the belief that other people's good fortune took away from my good luck. I believed that when others succeeded or were blessed, somehow I was deprived. As a result, instead of celebrating other people's blessings, I resented them.

Being thankful has helped me shift this misguided belief. Now when someone close to me experiences prosperity in whatever form, I see it as proof that the same success is possible for me as well. I know that whatever happens in the physical realm for one is replicable for all of us. I also now understand that when I begrudge another's good, I am effectively closing the door to my own good. There is no room in my heart for both resentment and gratitude.

Accentuate the Positive

By appreciating people, we are also able to change the way we see them. Jacqueline Bascobert Kelm, in her book *Appreciative Living,* talks about how we can change our relationships with others and ourselves by finding the positive core in the people in our lives. When we judge or criticize others, we unleash a slew of toxic emotions and chemicals into our minds and bodies. We stop our good short. But we can change this pattern by finding qualities to appreciate in other people.[8]

This does not mean that we have to agree with them or spend a lot of time with them. But when we can recognize that there is good in everyone and give thanks for it, we feel better. We relax and start to enjoy life more. We become more creative and more energized, and we attract people who want to assist us with our dreams. We are also now available to people we may have dismissed in the past because we were too busy judging them. And who knows what gifts or support they have for us? Since we see them differently, we can avail ourselves of the help they have to offer.

In her other book, *The Joy of Appreciative Living*, Kelm describes how it is almost impossible to make changes from a place of bad feelings. She explains that negative emotions can be an impetus to initiate change, but they don't motivate us for long. That is why she encourages people to change their outlook about a challenging situation by finding things they appreciate about it.[9]

As I explained in Chapter 5, on forgiveness, we actually make ourselves dumber when we harbor negative feelings. When we can find things to be grateful for in any situation, we bolster our energy and increase our capacity to think and imagine. We gain more confidence and clarity and can then make decisions that will make us happier, more effective people. And this is where we must start in order to replicate what Jesus did.

When I practice gratitude as taught by Jesus, I open the door for God's abundance to bless me. I prepare the groundwork to be able to receive more of God's riches. I no longer look at what I have and see it as lacking. Rather, I see it as evidence of God's abundance.

The most important aspect of practicing gratitude is not what it will possibly get me in the future; it is the way it enriches my current experience and enables me to give back in kind. When I give thanks, I am fully present. I am less likely to wish things were different. I no longer rob myself of the joy that is available to me now. When I practice gratitude, I see life's richness and beauty as it is in this moment. I balance the tension between my desires and my current outer reality without feeling deprived or neglected if my wishes are not fulfilled right away.

When we choose to follow Jesus' model of gratitude in all circumstances, we connect to the very fabric of God. We, too, then become open and willing vessels through which God can work. We develop a sense of humility, which I will talk about more in the next chapter. But for now, know that as we cultivate gratitude, we develop a sense of awe and wonder. We see how there are forces at work that are much bigger than we are, and we come to trust those forces. We give thanks in advance, as Jesus did, because we have cultivated his same level of faith. Like the other practices, gratitude is truly a powerful way to connect to our source and to know God as Jesus knew God.

Practicing the Practice

1. Let's start with an easy one: Take a moment and simply repeat the words "thank you" over and over again. Feel how your entire system shifts and relaxes. Feel how any fear you may be holding seems to melt away. Through that simple act, you can feel the power in the practice of giving thanks. Use these simple words as a mantra during your meditation time or when you find yourself heading down the path of destructive thinking.

2. Charles Fillmore, in his book *Prosperity*, suggests blessing everything. Bless the water you use to brush your teeth. Bless your clothes as you put them on, and bless the food as you prepare it. As you drive or walk down the street, send a silent blessing to each person you meet. See their beauty and send a message of appreciation for their presence. Remember that to bless means to confer abundance upon. Begin to notice how your attention shifts from doom and gloom to a sense of hope and possibility. As you create

the feeling of gratitude and appreciation, you open your heart and mind and see reasons to be grateful. You see the beauty and grace in your world.

3. Make gratitude lists. Most evenings, I take time to write down the things I am grateful for that day. I feel especially connected when I take the time to include details and specifics. Doing this embeds the event in my memory and body and causes me to appreciate the experience fully. If I don't have time to write the details, just bringing to mind the people or events that have blessed my day is a powerful way to fertilize my consciousness in order to experience life more deeply.

4. Practice giving thanks during the difficult times. Consciously look for the gift, and remind yourself that God is present and active in all things. Demand to see the blessing in the situation. It is there, I promise.

5. Practice being a gracious receiver. Spend an entire day acting as if everyone you encounter is there just for you. Appreciate each person's presence and his or her gift to you, no matter how seemingly insignificant it may be. Open your heart and allow yourself to receive that person's love and gratitude for you.

6. Learn to celebrate another's good fortune, particularly that of someone you have called an enemy. We stop our own flow when we begrudge someone else his or her good. We let our beliefs about our own lack and unworthiness color the situation. To counteract that impulse, send the person a note of congratulation on his or her success. In your

mind's eye, see that person's success as evidence that abundance is available for you as well. See someone else's success as your success.

Do Greater Things

-7-

Humility

It would have been impossible for Jesus to do what he did if his ego had been in control since arrogance would have undermined everything he attempted. Humility, therefore, was another key ingredient in his success. Free of ego and assured that God was the source of his power, Jesus humbly submitted to Spirit in order to be used in ways that would dramatically affect those around him.

What is humility? It has had a mixed reputation. We may think that it is a good thing; we just may not necessarily believe that it is good for us. We typically perceive humble people to be morally superior and yet meek—generally a description reserved for people who qualify for sainthood. We may believe that humility costs too much.

One look at the list of synonyms the thesaurus gives us— words like *self-effacing, subservient* and *inconsequential*—confirms that a humble attitude may not be all that desirable. After all, humility seems to be synonymous with being weak or a pushover. It means that somehow you are at the mercy of the world. In today's "every person for himself" environment, who wants that?

But when we read the New Testament, we do not see a picture of a subservient Jesus. According to the Gospels, Jesus was strong and confident and did not cower before anyone. He was anything but inconsequential. His idea of humility was one of self-assurance and empowerment. His example shows us how humility is quiet strength and the right expression of power. It does not force its way; rather, it lets its example speak for itself. The humble exude a might that demands the respect of even the most ferocious fighter.

People also feel a sense of deep peace and well-being around someone who is truly humble. When I see the Dalai Lama interviewed on TV or read something he wrote, my whole system slows down and relaxes, and I don't even have to be near him to have this reaction. There is a spirit that emanates from him that speaks of serenity and confidence.

But by no means is the Dalai Lama a pushover. He is seen as a powerful influence both by those who revere him and those who consider him a foe. World leaders go to the Dalai Lama for guidance and insight into world affairs. And the leaders of countries like China see him as the enemy to be destroyed. Yet if there is anyone on the planet today who demonstrates the kind of humble presence and strength that Jesus showed 2,000 years ago, I would say it is the Dalai Lama.

The Strength in Humility

People who exemplify humility have a healthy dose of self-awareness. They can see their gifts and seek to develop them in ways that bless others. Many of us are afraid to admit that we have gifts. Fearful that people will see us as arrogant or as braggarts, we downplay our talents. We work so hard at subverting pride that we reduce ourselves and, consequently, our effectiveness. When we diminish ourselves, the power of God working through and in us is diminished as well.

Because we are unable to celebrate our gifts and as a result feel inferior much of the time, we begrudge the gifts and talents of others, afraid that their competency will make us look bad. A person of true humility celebrates the gifts of others because he or she understands that everyone's contribution is necessary for the well-being of the planet. A spirit of humility helps us see how each of us is unique, but not special in a way that excludes anyone else.

I know that I have often felt threatened by others who I saw as more capable than I was. I somehow believed that I had to compete against them for the good things I wanted, so I resented their gifts and talents. Then there were times when I believed that someone was less capable than I was, and I felt superior to that person. But the feeling was short-lived because I was sure that someone I considered to be better than I was would soon come along and knock me back down to size.

So we swing between the two extremes of feeling superior to others and believing that we are the lowest of the low. We are either special or nothing at all. False modesty and false pride are two sides of the same coin of pride, which is the opposite of humility.

Humility means that we no longer need to feel more special than someone else in order to prove our own value. We understand that we are equipped with a distinct set of talents, and at the same time we see how everyone else is also gifted and has a contribution to make. Practicing humility means validating others rather than seeing them as rivals to be beaten in some imaginary contest.

We have all been taught that pride is one of the seven deadly sins and often goes before a fall. We don't particularly enjoy being around prideful people. But upon closer examination, we see that pride is really a cover for someone who feels inadequate. False pride—the kind that causes trouble—is a result of believing that we don't make the grade. So we go overboard trying to compensate for our perceived weaknesses.

Think of someone you find obnoxious because of a know-it-all attitude or continual need to be noticed. Behind all the grandiosity, however, is a person who is unsure and probably afraid that he or she will not measure up in your eyes. Humanity's biggest fear is finding out that we are insignificant. This fear generates all kinds of arrogance, or false pride.

Such pride also results from the belief that we are responsible for our talents and successes. True humility is the ability to see that our gifts originate from a Source greater than us. We had nothing to do with the raw material. Our gifts were bestowed upon us, to be used in a way that enriches the lives of others as well as our own. Humility, then, is the acknowledgment that there is a greater power of good being expressed through us in our unique way. As our awareness of this grows, our confidence expands, along with our capacity to share ourselves and our gifts.

When we relinquish the need to be more special then anyone else, we see that everyone is entitled to the same rewards and blessings that we are. False pride takes pleasure in someone else's failures and weaknesses. True humility, on the other hand, acknowledges the strengths of others and celebrates their successes.

What Did Jesus Do?

But does being a Christian mean that we have to allow others to use and abuse us? The Gospels report Jesus telling us to turn the other cheek when someone hits us. How could we possibly subject ourselves to such humiliating treatment? But nowhere does Jesus present a model of a submissive slave or doormat. The Gospels give us a picture of a strong, bold man who backed down to no one.

There is a difference between humility and humiliation. Being humble does not mean allowing yourself to be abused.

∞

It does not mean that you stand by and suffer in silence. It means that you know your power as a spiritual being and act from it, naturally free from any need to demand authority.

Walter Wink—professor emeritus of biblical interpretation at Auburn Theological Seminary in New York City and past Peace Fellow at the United States Institute of Peace—in his book *The Powers That Be*, offers a different perspective on Jesus' instruction to turn the other cheek. He explains that with this teaching, Jesus was encouraging nothing less than revolution.

Jesus told us to offer our left cheek when we were struck on the right side. Logistically, in order to strike you on the right cheek, a right-handed person has to backhand you. Backhanding is an act meant to put the person in his or her place. Wink suggests that by offering the left cheek, you're demanding to be treated as an equal.[1]

This is a radical idea, and the context is one of nonviolent resistance to injustice. Yet it gets the point across. Jesus was not asking us to let others walk all over us. He showed that we can stand up to injustice and misuse of authority in a powerful way without resorting to violence.

Again, we can look to the Dalai Lama as our contemporary example. The Dalai Lama has lived in exile for more than 50 years. He has watched the spiritual culture of his country be decimated by the Chinese. He has a right to be angry and to want revenge, and yet his message continues to be one of love and nonviolence. He talks about how the Chinese are his neighbors and you don't want to fight with your neighbors. With a spirit of reverence and deep humility, he inspires people all over the world to rethink how they see their so-called enemy. He demonstrates what it means to love unconditionally and to offer compassion without reserve.

Jesus made bold statements about himself that reflected his power and authority. He had the audacity to say things like "I am the light of the world. Those who follow me shall know eternal life" and "I am the way, and the truth, and the life." He also said, "I am the vine and you are the branches," and "I will give you living water, where you will never thirst again." The Gospels are filled with these declarations of power and certainty.

Jesus understood his capacity to bring about change. He could speak with such authority because in his humility, he knew that he was not the one doing the works. Rather, he knew it was "the Father within." To deny his power would be to deny God.

Jesus knew that his physical form was not the end-all. He knew, as no one else did, that he did not stop where his skin ended. Jesus had a deep awareness that he was the extension of the Father/Mother. He could see that the only way God has to express itself here in our world is through us. Jesus was able to go beyond a simple intellectual understanding to a deep experiential knowing of himself as God expressed in human form.

We get hung up on believing that this experience was unique to Jesus. Our self-deprecation keeps us from identifying with who Jesus was and what he did. Again, this is false modesty and wreaks havoc on our ability to repeat what Jesus did. In this moment, right now, commit to changing this worn-out perspective so that you can see yourself as Jesus needs you to see yourself.

We must be humble enough to admit that God has the power to express itself through anyone, including us. God's goodness is greater than our perceived badness, and God can use the least of us. We must humbly see ourselves as God's channel for light if we are going to repeat what Jesus did.

Jesus told us not to hide our light under a bushel but to hang it where everyone could see it. We are not to hoard it or pretend that it is not there, but rather share it in a way that will illuminate the dark corners in our lives and the lives of those around us.

Being humble does not mean that we deny our humanity. In fact, it means having the ability to see our very human traits objectively. We recognize our shortcomings for what they are without letting ourselves get caught up in the cycle of unworthiness and shame. The Dalai Lama has admitted that he still gets angry, but has also shared that the practice of awareness and compassion changes the anger into something positive.

Humility gives me the ability to see that God can work through me despite my very human ways. In fact, that is what makes the process so powerful. God can use my humanity in a way that serves others and reflects the Divine. This is not an ego trip that leads me to say I am great and wonderful. It means acknowledging a power much greater than my own small self and turning myself over to that power so that I, too, can be an instrument of God's grace.

Jesus deliberately and systematically returned our attention to the source of his power. He taught us by word and deed that his ability came from a source greater than he. He called his source the Father, and he had an intimate relationship with it. He showed us that the more we develop an image of God that we can trust, the more we surrender to the power of God and allow it to be expressed through us in grand ways.

Once again, we can see this in the Gospels. There are several places where Jesus proclaims who his source is. In John 5:30 he tells us, "I can do nothing on my own. As I hear, I judge; and my judgment is just, because I seek to do not my own will but the will of him who sent me." There was no doubt in his mind that he was there to serve God and humankind. He knew that anything he accomplished was a result of his allowing God to be expressed through him.

When we are aware of the power we have and we know where it comes from, we serve with love, even at the risk of looking weak. Jesus demonstrated that the humble carry a natural authority that allows them to be vulnerable, rather than having to maintain power by distancing themselves from others. True power lies in our accessibility and our ability to serve in seemingly demeaning ways.

One of the most dramatic illustrations that Jesus gave us was the time he washed his disciples' feet, which is depicted in the Gospel of John 13:4-11 in the Last Supper scene. All of the apostles were present and arguing over who was going to be the most important to Jesus when they got to the kingdom of heaven. They wanted Jesus to tell them which one would be the greatest and have the privilege of sitting at his right hand. Each was sure that he was more important than the others.

Jesus listened to them and then, without a word, removed his clothing, got down on his knees and went to each apostle to wash his feet. He took a basin of water and gently washed away the grime of the day. Peter was so taken aback that he initially refused to let Jesus clean his feet. He could not imagine his master in such a subservient position.

Jesus told Peter that he must allow it if Peter was going to follow him. He must see the example of true strength and power in service to another. After finishing, he got up, threw the water away, put his clothes back on and told them to do the same act for one another.

The message is obvious. Jesus wanted us to see that true greatness comes from our ability to act from love rather than superiority. We demonstrate true humility when we honor the sacred in one another. It takes a truly powerful person to serve others in a potentially demeaning way.

Life Journeys

I did some volunteer hospice work for a while as a requirement for my ministerial training. My job was to provide meals for patients and their families, and through this simple task I was forever changed. Going in with the attitude that I was doing them a great service by gracing them with my time and energy, I came away far more blessed, and educated, by each family than they were by me.

I watched the dying greet each day with grace and humility. They met me at the door with shaved heads, withering bodies and apologies for not being able to eat certain things because of their failing digestive systems. Each patient, in his or her own way, demonstrated courage, vulnerability and deep gratitude for life that day. They did appreciate my gift, the same way they appreciated being able to simply inhale and exhale. For many of them, life had come down to living a single day, and I got to be a part of their daily rhythm. It allowed me to put areas of my own life into perspective. With humility, I witnessed life simultaneously at its rawest and richest.

In the book *How, Then, Shall We Live?* Wayne Muller, founder of the neighborhood-philanthropy organization Bread for the Journey, told the story of his friend Kenneth, who was dying of AIDS. One day Kenneth told his nurse, Betsy, that he wanted to go outside, but Betsy insisted that he needed to stay in bed. Not to be deterred, Kenneth made his way to the door and out onto the lawn, where he collapsed.

Betsy ran out the door after him, afraid that he would hurt himself.

She found him lying on the grass, smiling. Kenneth had been reduced to a pile of broken humanity on his front lawn, and yet in that instant he was able to feel deep gratitude for the warmth of the sun on his check. Muller shared with humility how in that moment, life for Kenneth was reduced to this simple act of enjoying the warm sun on his face.[2]

Along the same lines, I recall watching the movie *Wit*, in which a woman was dying of cancer. She was surrounded by doctors discussing her case in a way that left her feeling invisible. They talked about her in terms of her illness, reciting the facts and statistics. Not one of them referred to her by her name or asked how she was doing. Once they had left the room, she was faced with the fact that she was utterly alone with her illness and impending death. All of their education and knowledge could not bring her the comfort she longed for.

Then the nurse came in. Less educated and less knowledgeable than the doctors, she offered the woman what the doctors with their vast knowledge could not: comfort. She took the woman's hands and began to rub them with lotion. Her touch and presence gave the dying woman the reassurance and companionship she was asking for. That is humility. When we let go of our need to impress and simply become present for those around us, we give the gift of Spirit.

Humility

Humility is the ability to stay connected to the humanity within us while pursuing our Father's business.

Humility also means being able to acknowledge that we cannot appreciate the full power of God. We arrogantly want to believe that we can comprehend everything because, if we can understand something, then we can control it. But some things are bigger than we are. Humility allows us to appreciate the presence of mystery and beauty in all circumstances. We may not understand how God works, but we realize that we do not need to understand; we learn to trust the presence of God and to see how we are its instrument.

Humility keeps us teachable, which means we continue to evolve. It also means we have the capacity to admit when we are wrong, adjust our opinions based on new information, and admit that we may not have all the answers. When we function from a belief in our own infallibility, we leave no room for others' opinions. We have to protect our own position, and the conversation breaks down. Enemies are manufactured, and peace is replaced by war. But when we see that there are other ways of looking at things, we create an environment of possibilities.

Our world recently saw what it means to let go of a sense of absolute certainty when President Barack Obama announced that the United States would ease travel restrictions to Cuba for Cuban Americans. With an air of power and humility, he acknowledged that completely cutting ourselves off from Cuba only aggravated a tense situation instead of helping us work toward healing. He did not say that we would be at the mercy of its dictatorship, but that we would relax some long-standing policies in order to make life easier for its people and their relatives here in the United States.

In response, Cuba's leader said that everything was on the table for discussion. We don't know where this will lead, but it is a powerful example of what can happen when we let go of the need to insist on our way. And no matter what our political beliefs, it will be interesting to watch how the situation unfolds.

Humility also means having the capacity to be awed and to experience wonder. A couple of years ago, my husband and I vacationed in the Canadian Rockies. On our way to Jasper, Alberta, we stopped to explore several glaciers along the highway. As we scanned the desolate landscape, we could see the ravishing effects of the glaciers' sheer power and weight. We walked along a path that went over mounds of gravel that had been unceremoniously dumped by the ice. The ground looked as if someone had taken a putty knife and scraped away anything that lay in its path. There were areas that looked as though they would be devoid of life for hundreds of years to come.

But then we took a closer look and saw signs of life returning. Along some parts of the trail, flowers, grass and other plant life were cropping up in places that had been covered by ice just a few short years ago. We paused to pay homage to the unstoppable momentum of life gently returning to this barren land. We felt awed by the force of life that was present. We were humbled by the power of God reflected in that scene.

Humility is the epitome of vulnerability. When we are truly humble, we are wide open. We hide nothing. We are open about our gifts and our flaws. We are free with our emotions, and we express love with abandon. We have the ability to recognize and appreciate beauty and grace in the present moment.

I have an image of Jesus being fully present and available for the people around him. In my mind's eye, I see him sharing himself without hesitation or defense. He was not afraid to connect with people on a deep "heart level."

One reason Princess Diana was so beloved was her humility and vulnerability. She used her royal status to do good works and did not look to receive any credit. She approached people with an open heart and deep compassion. She touched and inspired the world with her graciousness, humble demeanor and desire to make a difference.

As you begin to incorporate the practice of humility into your daily life, you, too, will develop a sense of reverence and sacredness. You will see how you play a vital part in the unfolding of the whole. You will appreciate yourself as well as those around you. You will no longer hinder your own effectiveness with false modesty or debilitating arrogance. You simply are, and you offer yourself to serve God and humankind by sharing the talents that have been so freely given to you.

You will find that your relationships become more meaningful because you are able to accept and give thanks for what other people have to offer. You no longer see them as competition. You no longer need to jockey for position, because you can see that we all have a part to play. Consequently, you simply get on with the business of sharing God's love. You see others as your partners in creation.

As we practice humility, we accept who we are and what we have to offer, and give it without hesitation. As a result, we see how we are replicating what Jesus did. If we stay observant, we can begin to see how the world is being transformed as a result of our willingness to share our gift.

Practicing the Practice

1. Ask yourself what the word *humility* means to you. As with any practice, the first thing we need to do is to be aware of how we view a word or concept. You may find yourself resisting the practice of humility. If so, be gentle with yourself and remind yourself who your Source is. You may need to go back and revisit the image you have of God.

2. Look around you and think about who inspires you. Whom do you look up to and hope to emulate? Considering this question will help you embrace the idea

that you are teachable and show you how others have influenced your life. True humility means having the ability to admire others. In giving credit to those who have influenced us along the way, we realize that we did not get where we are on our own. We see how we are all living extensions of one another.

3. Take another look around and see who is watching you. We begin to foster the quality of humility when we realize that our actions affect others. Jesus asked us to do what he did. He taught and then sent his disciples out to spread his teachings. We also teach, by word and by example. So ask, *Who is watching, and what am I teaching?* You see the sacred circle of knowledge and wisdom being passed on. I know that one of the greatest ways I can honor my teachers is to pass on what they have so freely given me.

4. Close your eyes, and say the things that Jesus said—to yourself about yourself. Say, "I am the light of the world!" Now repeat it. Let that statement sink in to the very essence of your being. How do you react when you say this? Do you believe it? Do you feel that you are being sacrilegious? Really ponder the words of Jesus and hear them as your own. Say to yourself one more time, "I am the light of the world." Imagine how you have the power to bring God alive for others.

5. Take stock of your gifts and talents. Write down the things you do well. I know how to communicate with people. I am comfortable in front of crowds, and I express myself in

a way that people can understand. I also know that I am not the one doing the work; rather, it is the presence of Spirit working through me. An arrogant attitude would be to discount my gift. God did not create anyone without some gift to share. Your purpose is to bless and serve those around you. So what do *you* bring to the table to share with others?

6. Identify at least 10 positive qualities in yourself. If this is difficult for you, ask others to share what they see in you. Listen without interruption, and simply thank them for their input. Remember, it is not you. It is the power and presence of Spirit acting through you. To deny your gifts is to deny God and God's power to bless through you. As Jesus told us, we are here to do the will of the one who sent us. God did not send a flunky. You must recognize this in order to be effective, so let others share what gifts they see in you.

7. Also take stock of your weaknesses. A by-product of recognizing your gifts is an increased ability to see your weaknesses or flaws. You learn to see yourself as the multidimensional human being you are. The more you can accept and embrace yourself, the more you can do the same for others. As you soften your attitude toward yourself, you become more generous toward those around you.

8. When you find yourself insisting that you are right about something, stop and simply listen. Be willing to set aside assumptions and hear a different viewpoint. See the

person with whom you are fighting as your teacher, and hear what he or she has to teach you. You don't have to agree with this person. Just be open to another perspective and another possibility.

9. Foster a sense of wonder and awe. When we can recognize God's magnificence around us, we can see that there truly is a power bigger than we are orchestrating our world. Go outside and let yourself be amazed by Mother Nature. Take a walk, and look for what defies the odds. During a recent hike in the mountains, I was awestruck by the trees that were growing right on the face of the rocks on the edge of the cliff. Look for the evidence of something much greater than you. See it as evidence of the inexplicable power of the invisible.

Do Greater Things

∞

-8-

Community

As we practice our spiritual principles and make an effort to comprehend what Jesus taught, we can begin to apply the lessons daily. Our relationships are the central place to integrate our newfound insights. If we have been sincere in our practices up to this point, then we have already started making changes in the way we treat others, and our relationships are starting to improve.

Everything Jesus taught and modeled for us would be meaningless if it didn't benefit our interactions with others. When you think about it, most of our challenges and joys involve other people. But now it is time to go beyond the comfort of our immediate surroundings and examine how to apply these teachings to the worldwide community. As we grow in our understanding of what Jesus taught, we realize that we can apply his lessons to people around the world just as well as we can to those in our daily lives. Indeed, in order to repeat what Jesus did, not only must we apply his principles to both groups, we must also see them as one and the same.

It is obvious that Jesus was fully engaged in his communi-ty. The Gospels, rich with stories of him with his friends and family, describe how he was born into a primary community that gave him his culture and identity. Jesus then purposely created a second group to give him the assistance and sup-port he needed to complete his mission. That combined com-munity became the source of some of his greatest joys, along with some of his deepest pains. The members of his tribe shared his growth each step along the way.

But for many of us, creating authentic community doesn't come naturally. Our lives are so full of activities and distrac-tions that we consciously have to make time for our relation-ships. They are no longer naturally woven into our days. We pull into our automatic garages, enter our temperature-controlled houses, shut the door and turn on something that keeps us from having to interact with others. We check our e-mail while on the phone, watch television during dinner, and play DVDs in the car to keep our kids entertained.

Then there is the added component of living in the United States. Most of us were raised with the notion that it is the American way to be independent. We were taught to be self-sufficient, to depend on no one but ourselves. Consequently, even when we seek relationships, we keep a part of ourselves guarded and unobtainable. We long to connect, yet we are afraid. As a result, we live lives that feel isolated and disjoint-ed, and we're not quite sure where we belong or whether we belong at all.

We miss out on so much when we live this way. When we fill our lives with "busyness" while keeping people at arm's length, we deprive ourselves of the sweet experiences that come with being intertwined with others. We know intellectually that connecting is a good thing, yet we still resist being vulnerable. It feels too risky to expose so much of ourselves to someone else.

Part of the difficulty is that we view one another as separate. It has become popular to talk about how we are all one, yet it is a hard concept to grasp. After all, we can see that the person sitting over there in her own chair is separate from us. And what about the people we don't want to be one with? Can we pick and choose those we are one with, or does this principle apply to everyone?

Embracing an Ever-Smaller World

The next time you make breakfast, stop to consider all the hands that have touched your meal. There are the farmers who grew the food and the processors who prepared it for sale. The transporters brought it to your local supermarket for the cashier to scan it so that you could buy it and take it home.

Then there are the people who created the packaging, the advertisers who marketed it, and on and on. You get the picture. This is our world community, and even though we do not know all of the people who participated in the process and would not recognize them if we met them face to face, they exist.

The extent of our worldwide interconnectedness was illustrated in a program, *Black Blizzard*, that aired on the History Channel in 2008. It explained how the Great Plains dust bowl of the 1930s was created by farming practices carried out during the first two decades of the 20th century and documented the far-reaching effects the droughts and dust storms had on the region and throughout the country.

The U.S. government had encouraged folks to move to the high plains to farm. Thousands of would-be farmers poured into the region, hoping to find a new life. They began to plow the prairie grasses that had survived the cyclical droughts of the area and had held the dirt in place for millions of years. They proceeded to plant wheat, a fragile crop dependent on adequate rainfall. The plains experienced unusually wet weather for a number of years, and farmers were encouraged to plant more of the crop. And for a time, things went well.

But then the rains stopped. In the late 1920s and early '30s, the region received only half the amount of its regular rainfall, causing the crops to wither and die. But that was not the end of the story: Because the wheat did not survive and the hardy prairie grass had been plowed under, there was nothing to hold the soil in place in an area that is normally windy. For the next 10 years, this section of the country experienced what were known as "black blizzards." The winds gathered the unprotected topsoil and created huge storms of dust and silt that traveled countless miles.

These storms were so huge that they often traveled across the country and dusted cities as far east as New York and Boston. Our country suddenly became much smaller, and the businessman in New York had to change his shirt several times a day because it was filthy from the dirt of a Kansas farm. The city's community had expanded to include the family surviving on tumbleweed that blew outside their prairie cabin.

Our world has shrunk even more since then. One has only to read the headlines to see evidence of our monetary inter-dependence. The 2008 collapse of the U.S. stock market, a result of risky investment and lending practices, caused mar-kets round the world to go into a free fall.

What the banker does on Wall Street or Main Street now affects what happens to the goods a factory produces in China. It is all evidence that when Jesus talked of our neigh-bors, he was talking about our entire world population. We can no longer insulate ourselves from the rest of the world. We are all members of the same community and must learn to live together on this very small planet.

And as our world shrinks and becomes more diverse, many of us feel more threatened and view one another with suspicion. The paradox is that as we hunker down with those who look most like us and reject others who may be different, we create an even greater sense of separation, and our desire for connection becomes ever more elusive.

All of this makes Jesus' teachings even more relevant today. We live with the knowledge that our world may not be here for our children. It is a recent worry that no generation had to deal with before 1945, yet the solution is in the teachings of Jesus. When we follow his example and seek to live as he did, we create a global community of harmony and sustainability. Jesus meant for us to practice these principles in order to create a more just, loving world. Now is the time to bring such practices to light.

We do this by opening our hearts. We support one another by celebrating our successes and grieving our losses together. We recognize ourselves in one another and understand that we are all in this together.

Life Journeys

There is an airline I fly every chance I get, and I often wonder why it appeals to me so much. As a customer, I get no frills. I have to wait in line to get a seat because seating is on a first-come, first-served basis. The airline doesn't offer extra services like movies or meals. In addition, its planes are smaller than those of most airlines, so passengers have less room.

I gained insight into my appreciation for this airline when I was forced to fly another airline for a trip out of the country.

My husband and I flew coach on this particular airline, and the first difference I noticed was that passengers were called by rows, with first-class customers seated first. As we boarded, we walked past the wall that divided us and the privileged ones. I observed how this separation of the two cabins created a feeling of disconnection. It was disheartening to think that the airline wanted it that way. The effect spilled over into the coach section. We were just another group of people who had nothing in common other than the fact that we happened to be going to the same place.

The airline I prefer, on the other hand, has no first-class section; nor does it assign seats. But by having its passengers stand in line, this airline—wittingly or unwittingly—creates a subtle difference that brings this community of passengers together in a way that no other airline I know of does. Instead of letting the "special" customers go first, it boards the physically challenged and the elderly before anyone else. There is a sense of grace and tenderness as we cooperate with this act of caring for the most fragile and vulnerable members of our community ahead of ourselves.

The flight attendants announce when children are flying for the first time and mention championship teams that are on their way back from tournaments. They tell us about couples who are celebrating anniversaries and elders who are commemorating milestone birthdays. Every time I fly on this airline, I feel as if I have connected somehow with all of these people. I am not just another person going to the same destination. I am part of a mini-community in which I get to celebrate my fellow travelers and be touched by their presence for this short time.

What Did Jesus Do?

Every time we connect with others this way, we touch our own humanity. We see how similar we are. We are more likely to view them with compassion and less likely to do them harm. We see our families in their families, our life experiences in theirs, and our futures as one. And it just feels better to live this way.

When we strive to apply what Jesus taught about living in community, we discover that we give to ourselves what we give to others. Pay attention to how you feel inside the next time you criticize or judge someone. My hunch is that you don't have a warm and fuzzy feeling; rather, your insides are probably tight and tense. In Chapter 5, I addressed how our bodies are affected when we harbor stressful, unloving feelings. By the same token, when we offer love and appreciation, we reap the benefits from those feelings because we experience them ourselves.

Jesus also told us that as we judge, so we will be judged. It is that old adage, "You spot it, you got it." We also act as mirrors for one another, reflecting our own and others' greatest strengths and weaknesses. What we see in others—the good, bad and ugly—we contain in some measure within ourselves. We begin to see that our reaction to another's behavior is simply an arrow directing us back to those things in our-selves that keep us small and limited.

Going even further, Jesus showed us that as we connect with one another, we connect with God. When we see God in the faces of those around us, every interaction becomes a holy one. In essence, we put skin on God. As a result, we become mindful of our actions because we realize that as we do to another, we do to God.

Living in a community gives us the opportunity to apply what we learn to our daily lives. For example, when we feel criticized by someone, we can either become defensive and retreat or we can practice what Jesus taught about loving our neighbor as ourselves and move toward our perceived enemy. We have that split second to decide how to respond to an attack.

Most of us will respond initially by retaliating, becoming defensive or withdrawing. But we can deepen what we have learned by practicing the tenets of love, acceptance, under-standing and strength as taught by Jesus. We take his lessons from the head and plant them in our hearts when we practice within our communities. Jesus lives through us when we choose to respond to others with love. And we, in turn, expe-rience the peace that he promised.

As a result we are also free because we are no longer vic-tims of someone else's behavior. We don't have to respond with hurt, anger, betrayal or any of the other myriad feelings that separate us. We practice what Jesus taught by seeing the best in others when they are not able to see it in themselves. We discover that nothing is lost by offering compassion; rather, everything is gained.

As we grow and mature, we also learn to appreciate all the members of our community—even those who challenge us. We learn to see them as teachers rather than as adversaries. I once heard a story about a group of people who had gathered at a retreat center to learn how to be peaceful. There was one cantankerous older gentleman who constantly complained and criticized, didn't pull his weight and was generally a pain in the neck. His presence made the experience miserable for everyone else.

At one point during the retreat, he had enough and decided to go. All of the participants silently cheered at his departure. But the director of the retreat went after the old man and offered to pay him to return to the community. He understood that lasting peace does not come from having our environment free of difficult people; rather, it is imperative for us to learn how to live in harmony with those who test us.

Such people challenge us to reach deep inside and discover our authentic selves. They become a catalyst for our growth. Think of the grain of sand that works its way into an oyster. The oyster takes the irritant and creates something beautiful. People we consider irritating work their way into our hearts until their presence polishes the pearl of our being. But this occurs only if we intentionally practice what we have learned.

Community

Abraham Lincoln told a story of how he was walking out in the country one day and came upon a farmer plowing his field with his mule. There was a whopper of a horsefly on the rear flank of the mule, and Abe went to shoo it away. The farmer stopped him and told him to leave it be. When Abe asked why, the farmer replied that the mule needed the aggravation to keep going.

As we learn to appreciate others in our community, we learn to see the best in ourselves. As we have discussed before, it is sometimes difficult for us to recognize and accept our own worth. But in fact, we reflect our own gifts back at ourselves when we identify them in others. If I see generosity, creativity or strength in you, it is because I have those same qualities—even if I am not aware of it yet.

There is a story in Matthew 16 in which Jesus asked his disciples to tell him what others were saying about him. Each of them shared what he had heard said about who Jesus was, but none of them gave him the answer he was looking for. None of them were able to grasp what he had been teaching and modeling for the past several months.

Disappointed in their responses, yet not one to give up, Jesus asked again: "Who do you say that I am?" Peter, excited, got a glimpse of what Jesus had been talking about all along. He exclaimed, "You are the Messiah, the son of the living God" (Matthew 16:16). You can almost hear Jesus' sign of relief: *Finally, someone is getting what I have been trying to explain all along!*

⌒

Jesus was hardly able to contain his excitement. He knew that the only reason Peter was able to recognize Jesus' true identity was that at some level, Peter realized in that moment that he, too, was the Son of the Father, divine in nature. Peter recognized something in Jesus that was in him as well.

That's how it works for us. We see the best in one another so that we can see and value it in ourselves. In that way we develop and use our gifts intentionally in order to contribute to our world.

The Dangers of Exclusion

Our communities are where we learn to accept love by letting other people love us. So many people have shared with me over the years how they have trouble doing this. They don't like the feeling of being vulnerable before others and are afraid of letting them down. But when we stay engaged with other people, we learn to let their love in and soften our hearts. We begin to trust that we are worth loving.

Our communities are also where we learn to love. I have read studies in which babies who were not given love did not develop normally, and many of them died. Eric Butterworth suggested that it was not because they did not receive love but because they didn't have the chance to give love. We are created to love, and unless someone is there to receive our love, we can never fulfill our potential. When people accept our love, they affirm that our presence matters and that the world needs our contribution.

A woman in one of my classes once shared how she struggled with feelings of inadequacy and doubted that she had anything to offer. She could give money—that was easy—but she didn't see what she personally had to contribute. I sat back and let members of that class share how her presence served them. They told her how they felt supported by her and appreciated her honesty and vulnerability. They expressed how they would feel that something was missing if she were not there. You could see the change in the woman as she took their words in: Her face softened and her body relaxed. She began to entertain the possibility that she did matter and that it was possible for people to love and appreciate her.

But not everyone gets this kind of validation, and those who don't may feel rejected and disenfranchised. Out of sheer desperation and anger, they sometimes retaliate with violence and destruction. We can see this in groups and individuals who have been marginalized in some way. Experts say that kids join gangs because they want to belong. They cannot see a place for themselves at the table with the rest of us, so they have no sense of purpose or possibility. They manufacture an often violent and lethal group to embrace—at the expense of their future, their freedom and often their lives.

We can also see how acts of evil happened in major historical events because people felt banished from the world. They could not see where they belonged. World War II and 9/11 are both examples of extreme exclusion gone disastrously bad. What if, somewhere along the line, humanity as a whole had paid attention to what each group was asking for and had found a way to respond to that need with love? Whether or not their position is justified, people create victims only when they feel victimized themselves.

Clinical psychologist and founder of the Center for Nonviolent Communication Marshall Rosenberg, in his book *Nonviolent Communication,* shared how he defused potentially dangerous situations simply by being present for the human need underlying every act of violence and destruction.[1] This does not mean that we condone such actions. But unless we are willing to see that the people committing them are crying out for love and inclusion, we will never create or experience the peace that Jesus describes for us in his teachings.

It is up to us to do our part to help each member of our community see his or her value. A young man once asked Mother Teresa how he could help her with her mission. She told him that the best way he could serve was to go out into the streets and find someone who was alone and disenfranchised and convince her that she mattered.

We get the chance to do this every day with the people in our lives. We do it by paying attention to them and seeing them for who they are. Don't discount the difference your attention makes in someone else's world. You can make an impact simply through your presence and consideration.

Within the community, we also learn the necessity of cooperation in order to take the next quantum leap. Rev. Michael
Dowd, in *Thank God for Evolution*, wrote about how different
kinds of bacteria came together to form the first cells with a
nucleus, and how small tribes of prehistoric people co-
operated to form agricultural communities.[2] Barbara Marx
Hubbard, in her DVD *Humanity Ascending*, talks about what
happened when a species reached a point of saturation in
which the environment no longer supported it: Its members
survived by cooperating with one another and another
species, resulting in the next stage of their evolution.[3]

We don't have to wait until we reach a desperate point to
start cooperating. The difference between us and other
species is that we have the intelligence to see the consequences of our actions and can project what will happen if we
continue a particular course of action. Having this ability
means that we also have a responsibility to question the status quo.

A Place to Make Your Voice Heard

As we observed in the "Practicing the Practice" section of
Chapter 2, on vision, Native Americans have a tradition of
asking how a decision will affect children seven generations
out. They understand that their actions today will have an
impact on their community in the future. When we choose
love, not only do we feel better and our relationships
improve, but we also act in ways that are healthy for the

planet. We experience less fear and anxiety and make wise, loving choices that ensure the sustainability of life here on earth. We cultivate the ability to stop and ask how a decision will affect the planet generations from now.

' We must also be willing to challenge injustices when we see them. The abuses we heap on one another only separate us further, making inclusion and cooperation almost impossible. Jesus was not afraid to question the social and religious practices of his day. In fact, he did this so often that he was seen as a revolutionary. He felt compelled to point out the inequality between the classes and how the vast majority of people were being crushed under so many rules and regulations. They were not living—they were barely surviving. He kept at it even when he knew that his actions were putting his life in danger.

History is replete with examples of brave souls who stood up to injustice. When Dr. Martin Luther King Jr. gave his "I Have a Dream" speech on August 28, 1963, he dared to list the sins of white America against its black citizens. He laid out a vision wherein his children would be judged not by the color of their skin but by the content of their character.

Thousands heard his words that day. Seeds were planted, and change was under way. A vision whose time has come cannot be stopped. He spoke to his community and we responded. Forty-five years later to the day, Barack Obama accepted the nomination for president from his party. He went on to win the election, becoming the first African-

American man to rise to the most powerful position in the world.

This cultural change was the result of the hard work and commitment of people all over the country making big and small changes every day in the way they treated one another. More and more people became increasingly uncomfortable with the discrimination that black Americans faced, and changes began to happen. Those fighting injustice were often met with resistance and violence, but evolution cannot be stopped. We still have a long way to go, but we as a nation have experienced a paradigm shift that will continue to resonate for years to come.

As we work toward eliminating injustice, we all benefit because we are free to share our gifts. When anyone is oppressed in a community, everyone suffers. When we focus on oppressing others, we are diverting energy and resources that could be used to enhance the world. Conversely, when we work toward including everyone, all of us experience a greater sense of freedom and expansion.

Remember, our community serves as a mirror into ourselves. When we open our eyes to suffering and injustice, we see our own suffering. We understand how we all long for the same things and experience the same losses. We see ourselves reflected back in the eyes of those whom we have dismissed. One reason Barack Obama succeeded in his bid for president was that people of all backgrounds saw themselves in him.

They looked beyond the color of his skin and saw their own humanity reflected back to them.

As members of a community, we also witness one another's pain. That is why 12-step programs are so successful. Members pay attention to others' stories and see their own struggle. Witnessing the suffering of another person while acknowledging our own pain is a powerful balm that also helps us learn to express empathy and compassion. The more we get in touch with our own pain, the more sensitive we are to the pain of others and the more accessible we become. Then real healing on all levels can happen.

Jesus modeled this for us in raising Lazarus from the dead. When he returned home to find that Lazarus had died, he wept with grief. He wept at the sadness that his friends and family felt and at their misdirected belief that they can be separate from God's eternal life. He shared the human experience of loss and sadness, easing his loved ones' pain and encouraging them on their road to healing.

By the same token, our communities are places to share our joys. I love the story of *A Christmas Carol* and Ebenezer Scrooge: A miser, he was often alone in his cold, dark office, counting his money. He was miserable even with all of that material wealth. Because he had denied himself his community, he became spiritually and emotionally bankrupt.

On Christmas Eve, Scrooge was visited by several ghosts, one of whom gave him the chance to see his past in its stark reality. He witnessed how he, bit by bit, had shut himself off from his loved ones. Another ghost showed him the lonely, unmourned death that awaited him as a result of his actions toward others. When he woke up Christmas morning, he realized that he had been given the precious gift of a second chance, which he grabbed for all he was worth.

We always have this choice. You have the choice right now to withdraw or to engage. But if you choose the path that Jesus laid out, withdrawing is impossible. His path demands that you participate fully in your community. So I invite you to do that. See yourself as an active participant and more—as a catalyst for awakening and transformation.

Practicing the Practice

1. Many of the practices included in the other chapters will automatically help you become more aware of your community. The practices in Chapters 2, 5, 6 and 7 in particular will help you foster a sense of community. I encourage you to revisit those sections with an eye to participating in your community.

2. You can also foster a sense of community by paying attention to how interdependent you are with other people. Silently give thanks to the folks who helped to make possible things such as your meals, clothing and housing. Get specific and thank the person who grew your food or sewed the buttons on your shirt. Humbly acknowledge the presence of these people in your life and how your day is better because of them. You can extend this process by

giving special words of appreciation to your waiter, cashier or mail carrier. Then pay attention to how your interactions with others change. Know that you are also energetically changing the consciousness of the world with these simple acts of blessing.

3. Celebrate and pray with members of your community. Notice how you feel when you see a newlywed couple go by or an ambulance with someone's loved one heading toward the hospital. Take a moment and send these people silent blessings. One of the endearing things about the town I live in is that traffic stops when a funeral procession passes. It is our way of acknowledging a life and those who are grieving the loss of a loved one even though we didn't know him or her personally. Offer that acknowledgment to someone else today.

4. Give each person you are speaking with your full attention. Turn away from the computer screen, the TV or your BlackBerry and concentrate 100 percent on what he or she is saying. If you feel especially adventurous, seek out someone who is isolated and give the gift of your time.

5. Get into the habit of looking at how your decisions today will affect generations in the future. Become more mindful of how your actions do affect the greater whole.

-9-

Death

In John 10:10, Jesus said, "I came that they may have life and have it abundantly." Everything that Jesus said and did directed our attention to life. Yet death—his death—is the backdrop for everything we know about Jesus. No one knows for sure if he knew he was going to be executed; yet it is nearly impossible to read his words and see his actions except through the lens of his death and consequent resurrection. It is a key part of his teaching that we cannot ignore, so I have included death as a spiritual practice.

Talking about death as spiritual may seem a bit strange, especially since our culture keeps death at a distance. But the messages of death and resurrection are central to our Christian tradition. Christianity is the only major religion whose leader was executed. This fact fundamentally informs who we are as followers of Jesus and is as much a part of our conversation as the miracles, or at least it should be.

It is not that we don't talk about Jesus' death. We do, as demonstrated by our fascination with movies like Mel

Gibson's *The Passion of the Christ*. Drive to any small southern town during the summer, and somewhere you can see the *Passion* play performed in an outdoor theater. But that is not where Jesus wanted us to focus our attention. When we look at his death this way, it becomes a distraction rather than a teaching tool and an example.

Adopting death as a spiritual practice means changing the way we perceive Jesus' death. We have relegated it to a special category, making Jesus unique and his end something beyond the ordinary. Often his execution is seen as predestined and, as discussed earlier, necessary for our salvation. We have created an entire mythology around his demise and the subsequent events. But in doing so, we miss its essential message.

The reality is that Jesus died for the same reason thousands of others did during his day—for protesting against the powers that were in control. Jesus stood up to the injustices he saw, and he spoke out. He drew unwanted attention to himself and ultimately lost his life as a result. This is not to minimize his sacrifice. But when we make Jesus' death special, we do an injustice to all the other people through the ages who died because they fought wrongdoing. Their murders were no less important or meaningful.

The difference between Jesus' death and theirs is the lesson we can gain from his experience. Through his violent death, he taught us that life is eternal, no matter what the physical evidence may say to the contrary. He modeled that death is the ultimate act of surrender, letting go and recognizing that God is so much more than what we can see on this material plane. He demonstrated for us that death cannot snuff out life. The eternal is what remains.

There is a story in Matthew (22:23-32) about the Pharisees questioning Jesus on the law. They asked him what would happen if a woman married seven brothers in a row and there were no children from any of the marriages. Who would be together in heaven? Jesus responded to them that they were looking for God among the dead. He told them that when they died, they would become like angels, and he admonished them to look for God among the living.

In other words, we all face the end of this life as we know it. If we look for God or heaven with our senses and limited perspective, we will not find it. In fact, we will twist ourselves up with crazy notions, such as this question from the Pharisees. But there is much more to life beyond what we can perceive. When we begin to grasp on some level how the essence of life is eternal, then we see that this physical reality is simply one way that God expresses life. We become less attached to the material things and more focused on what is true and unending.

In Life, Many Deaths

We face death on a multitude of levels at different stages throughout our lives. The most obvious lesson Jesus taught was about our physical deaths, yet his teachings apply to much more than just the end of our bodies. Death is designed into the fabric of our routines. Even when something good happens, something else must end in order to make room for the new condition.

Paul described this beautifully when he said, "I die every day" (1 Corinthians 15:30). Some aspect of us and of our world dies each day. At any given point, there is something changing or dying right before our eyes. Jesus spoke of the way the seed must die in order for it to bear much fruit. In John 12:24 he said, "Truly, truly, I say to you, unless a grain of wheat falls into the earth and dies, it remains just a single grain; but if it dies, it bears much fruit."

Every day we are required to let go of something familiar. It may be physical, but it may also be intangible, like a dream, or simply another day gone by that we will never have again. We may also find that beliefs we once held no longer work for us. As we grow, ideas become obsolete, and we are required to let go of what was once precious.

Recently a member of our congregation had a baby. She was so excited about the whole process and the gift that was coming into her life. But after her daughter was born, she struggled. She felt as though a chapter in her life was ending and a part of her was dying. Her independence was restricted, and she was now responsible for this little being. She grieved her image of herself as an unencumbered woman.

But instead of shaming herself for having these thoughts and feelings, she embraced the process by facing uncomfortable, often culturally unacceptable emotions. She talked with others about the way she felt, a process that gave her permission and space to mourn her previous lifestyle. Ultimately she realized that the image of herself without children had to die in order for the mother in her to be born. Today she is a doting parent, relishing the joys that her daughter brings to her.

We all face these kinds of deaths, which challenge us to look at our own perspectives on life, ourselves and God. And if we are willing, we can find deep spiritual nourishment in facing the death of each facet of our lives.

Let's examine this. In Unity we talk about life as eternal, and the resurrection of Jesus is our evidence for this. Yet here I am saying that death is real and is to be embraced as a spiritual practice. How can we reconcile the two?

As with so many spiritual ideas, this concept is almost impossible for us to understand if we see things around us as permanent. In fact, when we suffer under this illusion, we come to depend on what we can see and touch. We invest our time and energy in the people and circumstances that define our lives. We know intellectually that all of these things can disappear in an instant, yet somewhere in us we believe we are invulnerable and that things will remain the same.

Take a moment and look around the room you are in right now. Try to identify one item that will be there a million years from now. Nothing in the outer physical realm lasts forever. Yet everything you see, including you, came from an everlasting source. The material things around us represent the eternal nature and goodness of God. The chair you are sitting on right now was an idea in the mind of God that was manifested through humankind into the outer world. The idea was always there, waiting to be discovered. Ultimately, the chair came from the Infinite Source of all good. Your seat won't be here a million years from now, but the Source from which it came will be. Practicing death leads us to discover what is true and permanent. We loosen our grip on earthly illusions and discover the true riches of heaven.

Jesus chided his listeners on several occasions to watch their attachment to outer or earthly things. In Matthew 6:19 he told us not to store things on earth, where moths and rust can consume them, but to store them in heaven. He knew that true happiness and fulfillment were not to be found in stuff. And unless we are willing to accept the impermanence of the physical world, we will never understand this greater spiritual truth.

This sounds simple in theory, yet it is one of the most difficult and painful concepts to grasp. Case in point: our country's financial upheaval. Unemployment is high, housing prices have plunged, and the stock market is struggling to recover from the biggest collapse since the Great Depression. People are panicking because our way of life is dying.

By applying spiritual principles and the teachings of Jesus, however, we can view current events not as the end of everything but as the end of one era and the beginning of another.

Death

I don't want to minimize the trauma that is happening in the lives of millions of people around the world, but if we really believe what Jesus taught us about God, then we can trust that the status quo is shifting in order to make room for a more evolved way of living. But we have to let the old way of life die. And that is extremely scary and painful for most people.

Life Journeys

By embracing death as a spiritual practice, we also confront the perceptions that keep us from living life fully. We accept the invitation that life issues to face the death of paradigms that keep us trapped. When we do, we discover something much more enduring and powerful that expands life as we know it.

Recently I was with my dad as he went through surgery for a hip replacement. It was an elective procedure, and we expected an uneventful recovery. I made plans to be with him Sunday through Saturday, enough time to see him through the surgery and then get him situated in an assisted-living facility.

I could never have anticipated what actually happened. The anesthesia affected my dad profoundly. He became delirious and disoriented and kept forgetting that he had had surgery. He also became combative and had to be held down. I quickly became the parent in the situation.

When I got home and was able to get some distance from the situation, I found myself grieving deeply. For the first time, I saw the stark reality of what life might be like without my dad. It was as if someone had removed blinders from my eyes and I was seeing my dad as others saw him: a 78-year-old man with severe arthritis and beginning stages of dementia. It hit me hard that my dad would never be there for me the same way he had been in the past.

I felt our relationship as father and daughter dying, and I saw myself stepping into a new role with him that I didn't feel prepared for or want. Now I had not been dependent on my dad for anything other than moral support for several decades, but I realized that at some deep, fundamental level, I still saw my father as my safety net. I felt something within me slipping away as I came to grips with the change in his status.

But when I looked back on the week I had spent with him, I also saw that a miracle had occurred. The old image of me as a child dependent on a parent had shifted to that of a confident, assured and strong woman. I discovered that, when I was most tired and overwhelmed, I'd found a reservoir of strength upon which to draw. When I chose to be fully present to him and the changes that were happening, I felt a deep sense of well-being. In that instant, as my relationship with my father as I knew it died, I felt fully alive.

I remember clearly the exact moment a new relationship was forged. I had been called back to the hospital because he had ripped out all his tubes and had managed to get out of bed, broken hip and all. The nurse on duty asked me to spend the night with him to help look after him. I gathered my stuff, grumbling to my uncle, and headed back to the hospital.

It was about three in the morning, and all was quiet except for my dad. I had gotten up for the umpteenth time to put his oxygen tube back in his nose and push him back on the bed, when I was able to step out of myself and see my dad as another human being who needed comfort and care. In that moment, I knew my purpose was to be completely available for him, with no agenda about what I might get in return. I realized that my dad was no longer the man I had known and loved; something had shifted. But all that mattered was his well-being.

Amid all that pain and confusion, I saw with clearly what was important. In that moment, all of the past hurts, resentments and accusations died, along with our old relationship. I realized that my sole purpose was simply to be there for my dad. I was given a glimpse of what the eternal means. I saw that the fullness of God was there in the room with both of us as together we moved through that experience of death and resurrection.

What Did Jesus Do?

Jesus faced his own demons and won. He knew that he had doubts and understood that as a spiritual being living a human existence, he needed to root out those fears and lay them to rest in order to be effective in his mission. The story of his time in the desert—during which aspects of him died so that a more evolved Jesus could emerge—specifically illustrates the practice of death.

This period of death and transformation for Jesus started when John baptized him in the River Jordan. We read in Matthew 3:17 that right after John anointed him, Jesus heard God say to him, "This is my son, the Beloved, with whom I am well pleased." He knew with every fiber of his being at that moment that he was the substance of God in physical form. He understood that when people saw him, they saw the Father.

Yet he resisted this truth, as we all do. Aspects of his personality felt threatened by the change that was happening within him. Knowing that he had to face these internal forces, he took time away to confront the voices of doubt that he was hearing. The Bible tells us that he was in the desert for 40 days and 40 nights.

Metaphysically, the number 40 simply means that something takes as long as it takes. He may have been in the desert for a day, a month or the actual 40 days. The duration is not important. What is important is that he took time to face the aspects of himself that were interfering with his ability to be all that God had created him to be.

The story tells us that the devil appeared to tempt him toward the end of his self-imposed banishment, when he was famished, tired and ready to call it a day. Extremely weak and vulnerable, Jesus probably questioned what he believed and knew to be true. He was more susceptible to his fears and illusions than at any other time.

And that was the way he wanted it. It was his way of bringing the destructive illusions to the surface so that he could see them clearly. He understood that we must see something for what it is before we can let it go. He saw how harmful his limiting thought patterns and behaviors were. He knew that part of himself had to die in order for him to be fully alive.

The devil challenged Jesus' newfound awareness. He used a series of temptations to challenge Jesus' beliefs regarding whom he could trust and what was real. First the devil tested Jesus' belief about the source of his daily nourishment. He knew that Jesus was weak from not eating. So he dared Jesus to turn stones into loaves of bread.

This seemed like an easy-enough task for someone as evolved as Jesus, and what could possibly be the harm in it? But Jesus knew that it would be a misuse of power. He knew that the power came from God and that God was his supplier. He could make something happen, but it would be just that: He would be making it happen. He knew that if he allowed himself to be seduced into abusing his power, he would miss out on true nourishment. He would stop short of learning how to use the power of God within him to bring about real change for humanity. He also knew that God would provide for him once he had completed his process.

There are times when we all want to make something happen. In a particular situation, we may even have the power to force a change. We may get our physical needs met this way, but when we short-circuit the process to make something happen, we miss the nourishment that really counts—for our spirits. We perpetuate our fears and doubts about life because we did not give God a chance to demonstrate her power for us. When we take matters into our own hands, we diminish our spiritual power. Life becomes hard and gray.

But Jesus knew better, so he told the devil that humankind does not live by bread alone. We may get fed on the physical level, but spiritually we die a little each day because our diet lacks the spiritual nutrients we need to live an abundant life. Our true nourishment, which provides for all our needs, comes from God.

Then the devil—or, in metaphysical terms, that part of us that rejects God—challenged Jesus to climb a pinnacle and throw himself down to let the angels catch him. Jesus responded that we are not to put God to the test. We all want the big, dramatic proof that God is real and present in our lives. But when we test God, we don't believe; otherwise, we would not need to test the theory.

Jesus knew that the miracles, the transformations, come from taking tiny steps every day. Jesus also knew that God gives us intelligence and discernment that, when used, keep us safe and on the right track. For Jesus, jumping from that height would have been like our walking across the interstate at rush hour and asking God to protect us. When we need extraordinary displays of power, we lose the ability to see God in the everyday.

Jesus buried his need for spectacular manifestations of God's power and instead learned to see God in the routine. He saw that God was transforming him and his life, moment by inconsequential moment. He knew that as a result, he would be able to trust God more, in both the small details and the big events.

Finally, the devil, or the voice of illusion, challenged Jesus to claim all the power over the world. If he would worship all things physical, he could be the most powerful man in creation.

This kind of thinking is so seductive. If we have power, we have control, which means that we can manage our lives and avoid bad things. We may even think that we can keep death at bay. But Jesus discovered during his time in the desert that all power comes from God, and even if he had all the power in the physical realm, he would never have the power to avoid death. That came only from knowing God. So he buried the desire to seek power for power's sake in order to make God's power come alive in him.

Now the Gospels present this as one neat little story, with a beginning and an end. But that is not how most of us learn to trust God. For me, personally, it has been an ongoing process of awareness, death and rebirth: I discover a new principle. I see the places in my life that are out of alignment with the new principle. I go through the process of giving up the old way of seeing and doing things, or allowing it to die within me, so that the new lessons have space to take hold within me. Life then becomes a process of embracing the new, letting go of the old and living more fully.

The Taboo of Death ...

Let's take a closer look at physical death. Jesus spoke extensively about his own death. It was an integral part of his teachings, and he understood that it was an important part of his journey. He talked with the disciples about how he was going to go away, and when they asked about following him, he said that they were not ready yet. He knew at some level what was going to be asked of him.

The Gospels were written after Jesus' death and resurrection, so they were written through the lens of his death. It is impossible to know what he knew about his future—whether he knew the details of his death or if he simply understood the risk he was taking by speaking out the way he did. But we can see throughout his teachings that Jesus faced his death every day. It walked side by side with him.

Again, death is a taboo subject for those of us in the West. We in this culture want to sanitize death by using euphemisms such as "crossing over" and "slipping away." I have heard death referred to as "making one's transition." And technically that is what happens, but those words seem to deny that the person is gone from the physical realm. Why do we say it this way? Because we want to lessen the impact and thereby lessen the hurt. But the lesson that Jesus presented with his death is that unless people lean into death, they can never experience life.

One dysfunctional way that we have coped with the prospect of our own physical deaths is by constructing the concept of heaven. The Christian tradition developed the doctrine of paradise as a reward after we die for having lived a "good Christian life." This life thus becomes a stopover on the way to heaven. No longer are we living for today; instead, we are calculating how each act will affect our chances of getting that reward.

But when we do this, we are no longer present. We either regret the past or worry about the future. The doctrine of heaven diminishes the values and beauty of this life for a better one later on. Effectively, it kills life here.

Jesus did not teach about heaven being a place that we earn. Rather, he taught us that heaven is created when we learn to see God in all things. We manifest heaven when we relish life and delight in the commonplace moments. When we understand how the eternal nature of God is woven into everything, we understand the true meaning of heaven.

... And the Truth of the Resurrection

Jesus also taught us that life is much bigger than what we can see with our eyes. Death did not contain him; rather, it was the catalyst for his transformation and final awakening. Retired Episcopalian bishop and best-selling author John Shelby Spong, in his book *Jesus for the Non-Religious,* talked about how the disciples had an experience with Jesus after his death that was beyond anything they had known before. Something happened to them that they could not explain, something that changed them forever.[1] Marcus Borg called it a post-Easter experience.

The Gospels tell us how the followers of Jesus walked, talked and ate with Jesus following his resurrection. Whether that happened the way it was written, no one will ever know for sure. But these men and women became infused with the power and glory of God, and awoke to their capabilities to lead and create a movement that changed the world.

The experience was so powerful that they felt compelled to document it. The story grew as time went on. It became part of our story and the story of Christianity. But the facts got murky in order for the truth to be told. Marcus Borg, in his book *The Heart of Christianity,* has spoken of the way Gospel stories, and this one in particular, were not written to reflect facts. But embedded in every story is truth, and that truth resonates with us.[2]

The Easter story is a beautiful account of hope and resurrection. Death could not contain the spirit and power of Jesus. In Luke 24:1-7, the women who followed Jesus go to the tomb on Easter morning to tend to his body. When they get there, they find that the stone has been rolled away and there are two men sitting on top of the tomb in dazzling white clothes. These men ask the women who they are looking for, and the women tell them. Then they asked the same question that Jesus asked in Matthew 22: "Why are you looking for living among the dead?"

This is one of the most profound questions in the Bible, and it is applicable to all of us. We mistakenly believe that there is some magic cure-all outside us that will make us happy. We put life on hold until the special wish is granted. But that means we are not living fully. Parts of us become dead to ourselves and those around us.

When we bury the illusion that we lack anything, however, our true nature of wholeness, abundance, joy and eternal life is resurrected. And when it comes time to lay this body down, our true selves will continue to experience love, grace, beauty and all of the other attributes of God. Life is not restricted to this body. When we know this, we, too, will be able to willingly lay it down.

Jesus showed us how to find what is true in the midst of the dying or dead. He encouraged us to look for what is permanent in the presence of God. His example showed us that death is not something to be avoided. That is impossible. But we can discover how life exists side by side with death.

Death can never shut out the power and presence of God. No matter how painful the circumstances, the fullness of God is always present. But when we frantically try to keep things from changing, we miss that revelation. We see only the loss of something dear to us. We are impervious to the presence of God's life-sustaining power.

From the beginning of time, people have been trying to figure out how to live forever. They have tried just about everything, from looking for the fountain of youth to having their bodies frozen after death until a cure for their disease can be found. But do we really want to live forever?

In a 2005 issue of *What Is Enlightenment?* magazine (now called *EnlightenNext*), spiritual teacher Andrew Cohen, a pioneer of evolutionary enlightenment, talked with the philosopher Ken Wilber about the concept of eternal life. They discussed the possibility of living indefinitely because of medical advances. Wilber distinguished between immortality of the body, soul and spirit. When we refer to the body and soul living forever, we are talking in terms of linear time. We want the material world as we know it today to last indefinitely.

Cohen and Wilber concluded that living forever in the physical realm felt unnatural and out of sync with spiritual principle. When we speak from the realm of Spirit, we are talking timelessness. Wilber said, "For the realm of nondual spirit, immortality doesn't mean living forever. It means the experience of *timelessness*; it means a moment of pure timeless presence, not going on forever in time."

The two also addressed the way all that went before and all that is to come converge in this now moment. Wilber said, "You can have eternal life by simply and fully being in the timeless present with spirit, now." They concluded that once you accept the impermanent nature of this physical life, you will find the permanent experience of God.[3] In other words, when we learn to be fully present in the moment, we learn to live forever.

That is what Jesus discovered. He found the fullness of God in every moment, especially in the face of death. In fact, the only way we will ever know God's eternal and permanent nature is if we are willing to let our attachments to anything else die.

This is not easy. In fact, it can be excruciating. We are not convinced that God will replace what we give up with something so much better. We hang on to what we have with the tenacity of a bulldog, believing that our very survival depends on it. But in doing so, we never discover that God is fully present, even as we inevitably let go of what is most precious to us.

We must face it: Our bodies die, our dreams die, our relationships die, our loved ones die. The leaves on the trees, the flowers, the grass—everything we can see will end or die in some fashion. But when we see the reality of death all around us, we discover life and the immortal. We resurrect the life that God promised each of us.

So gather your courage and your dedication to the path, and add the spiritual practice of death to your routine. As you learn to embrace the impermanent aspect of life, you will discover what is true and eternal. As you become more present in each moment, watch as life then becomes richer and fuller.

Practicing the Practice

1. Take inventory of what you believe you cannot live without. What would happen if you lost your job, your spouse, your health or any other person or thing you hold dear? Journal about how life would look without these elements.

2. Then allow God to paint a different picture for you. Spend time in meditation, allowing the vision that God has for you to emerge. Journal about this too.

3. What do you believe about life and death? What do you believe will happen to you when you die? Does your belief help you live life fully now?

4. Practice mindfulness. Continue your meditation practice, focusing on your breath. This time, see it as a tool to help you be more aware of life in this moment. When you find yourself drifting away, bring your mind back to the eternal now.

5. Ask yourself if you would want to live forever. Why or why not? Is there anything you would experience by living forever that you could not experience in this moment right now?

6. Make a list of the principles and truths that are eternal. Contemplate those ideas and become mindful of them during your daily routine.

-10-

Service

All the work, all the practice and growth, comes down to this last spiritual discipline. Service is the sole reason for everything we have discussed and applied throughout this book. Actually, the sole purpose for our existence is simply to be happy. And we will never know true joy until we freely share our gifts, our time and ourselves.

Jesus discovered this powerful secret. He knew that his very reason for being was to share himself and his wisdom with those around him. Doing so was as natural for him as breathing because he understood that all fulfillment comes from giving oneself.

Jesus was also very specific in his instructions to us about service. He told us that whatever we do to the least of us, we also do to him. When we feed the hungry or help the sick and weak, we serve the Divine. When asked about helping our neighbors, Jesus gave the example of the Good Samaritan. Jesus told the rich, young ruler that the way to heaven was to sell his possessions and give them to the poor. His was a

Gospel of compassion and generosity, leaving no wiggle room to avoid service.

Many of us find this concept of service to be foreign or unattractive. As with several of the other practices I have written about, service is not always met with enthusiasm. It is an idea loaded with misperceptions and confusion. We have all been taught that service is a good thing, but it doesn't always feel that way.

We may think that service means hard work, with a promise for rewards at some undesignated time in the distant future. We may also have heard that service requires great sacrifice in order to be considered legitimate. Somehow, this beautiful practice has been turned into something to be avoided rather than pursued and celebrated. Case in point: A friend of mine recently shared that he was in a meeting where several people said they didn't like the word *service* because it implied being a servant, which seemed demeaning.

Jesus presented a very different picture of service. He showed us what happens as we mature spiritually: Our reasons for giving become more fully developed. We find ourselves serving, as he did, not to get something in return but because we recognize that giving is the essence of who we are, so we experience the joy that comes with it.

I know that I have to be aware of my own motives and be careful not to lose myself in service to others. In the past, I was afraid of disappointing people because I thought they had expectations I could not meet. Service was a tool I used to bargain for acceptance. I did it with an expectation that people would respond in a certain way, but they usually did not.

As a result, I overextended myself. I decided that what I had given was inadequate and felt driven to give even more. I often ended up feeling drained and resentful, especially when I didn't get the appreciation that had driven me to do something in the first place.

Yet there have also been those times when I gave of myself for the pure pleasure of giving. I saw a need and knew that I had something to contribute. I knew that I belonged in the world, and I saw how others benefited from my presence. And it just plain felt good to give so freely.

As I grow and mature in my spiritual practice, I become more aware that when I give service, I am involved in something much bigger than myself. It feels good to sit back and see that what I do makes a difference. I know I am not alone in this feeling. Deep down, we all yearn to know that we count in the lives of others and would be missed if we were gone.

When I share my gifts and my time, I become less involved with my own little agendas and am able to let go and trust more. My trust in God and in the goodness of life grows as I become more focused on others.

Jesus wanted us to experience the richness that comes from giving without expectation or motive. Service is not something we do to earn brownie points from God. This goes back to our conversation in Chapter 3, on faith. If we see God as something outside us, wanting us to be good, then we will see service as a way to bargain with God. It becomes our ticket to heaven. But when we adopt Jesus' perspective on service, we discover that service is a way to connect to the Divine in one another and ourselves.

Following Jesus means serving as he did. He could not help giving of himself; to deny giving service would have been to deny himself. When I hear people describing others as "good Christians," I often wonder what that means. Marcus Borg, in *The Heart of Christianity*, talked about Jesus' response when he was asked which commandment was the greatest: "You shall love the Lord your God with all your heart, and with all your soul, and with all your strength, and with all your mind; and your neighbor as yourself" (Luke 10:26-28).

According to Borg, when we love God, we love what he loves. Borg expands on this idea by stating that if we love God's beloved, then we accept what God has placed in our hands: responsibility for our brothers and sisters all over the globe. We no longer see the world in terms of what it can give to us but, rather, in terms of what we can give to it. This is what it means to serve.[1]

Before we go on, let's dispel a few myths that keep us from giving fully of ourselves.

Myth No. 1: Service Can't Be Fun

Somewhere along the line, we have heard that it doesn't mean much if we enjoy it. In fact, I have had people tell me that they can't count their service because they like it too much. Quite the opposite is true. Doing something out of obligation or in hopes of a reward taints the experience for everyone involved. We are unhappy and less productive, which infects the mood of everyone around us. We are doing more of a disservice than any good.

I once did some volunteer work for the library, going once a week and offering to do whatever needed to be done, which usually meant clerical work such as shelving books and otherwise helping the library stay organized.

I hated every minute of it. I wanted to strike up conversations with the patrons about what they were reading. I wanted to stop shelving and read what I had in my hand. I kept checking the clock. That job was the completely wrong fit for me. I realized that I may have been helping, but I was not being of service. Needless to say, I did not last.

This experience helped me learn that it was okay to enjoy the service work that I do. In fact, that was imperative if I was going to continue doing the work. I started looking at the activities that I did enjoy. I realized that I wanted to give at the library because I loved to read and talk about what I had read. I thought that working there would let me share my love for reading. I had the right place but the wrong job.

∽

I started facilitating discussion groups at the library on books that I liked. I am a presenter and teacher, and I used those talents to foster conversation among people and to encourage them to read. I thoroughly enjoyed my experience, and I got great feedback from the participants.

We serve best when we are involved with something that uses our gifts. Anytime we give from our passion, we give wholeheartedly and joyfully. Our enthusiasm is infectious, and people often join in because of our influence.

Myth No. 2: Service Means Sacrifice

We are mistakenly told that when we give of ourselves, we lose something, because there is only so much to go around. As a result, many of us ration what we give. But there is an interesting phenomenon that happens when we give without hesitation and with the right motives. We find that not only is there enough to go around, but we actually have excess. Somehow, when we focus on others, the universe expands by offering an overabundance of the very thing we are sharing.

I love to watch people discover the principle of tithing. I teach a prosperity course called "Keys to the Kingdom," by Religious Science minister David Owen Ritz, which invites people to try the spiritual practice of tithing for seven weeks. During that time, they commit to tithing 10 percent of their time to something or someone they believe in, 10 percent of their income to the place that spiritually feeds them, and 10 percent of their day back to Spirit by spending time in prayer, meditation and study.

The results are amazing. Time and time again, people report that they have money left over at the end of the month when previously they had been counting pennies during that last week. They share how they have extra time to do the things they love and bring greater focus and clarity to their other activities. As they learn to share freely of their time, talents and money, they demonstrate the principle that to give is to receive.

Through giving, we learn that we live in a lavish, generous universe that longs to express abundance through us. As we turn our attention to others, we find that we are no longer focused on what we can get. Consequently, we let go of the fear that there is not enough to go around. This frees our energy to allow more of God's grace into our lives. We have less need to control and manipulate our world, and we learn to trust the presence of divine order. Rather than asking us to sacrifice ourselves, true service blesses us in miraculous and unforeseen ways.

We may look at an activity someone else is involved in and shudder in horror, believing that it must be a huge sacrifice. But for that person, it may feel like the most natural, joyful thing in the world. In a 2009 report on *CBS Sunday Morning*, journalist Armen Keteyian introduced the audience to high school basketball coach Bob Hurley, who, many people might say, has made huge sacrifices for the boys at St. Anthony

High School in Jersey City, New Jersey. In the 37 years he has coached the basketball team, he has never earned more than $9,000 annually. But he has taken boys from a difficult neighborhood with virtually no resources and turned them into a team with an outstanding record.

The school doesn't have a gymnasium. The young athletes have to go to the local bingo hall to practice. But despite these conditions, Coach Hurley has been able to develop the boys individually and as a group. Of all the youths he has coached over the years, only three have not made it to college.

Because of his team's success, Hurley has been offered millions to leave St. Anthony's and coach college basketball. But he has turned down all offers. Before coaching, Hurley was a probation officer, a job that enabled him to see firsthand what happens to young boys who have no one to give them direction. He understood that the men he faced each day were products of the bad decisions they had made at age 13 or 14. That was when he knew he had to do something to help boys make different choices at that critical time in their lives.[2]

As I watched him being interviewed, I was struck by how happy he was. Nowhere in his countenance did I see a man resentful about missed opportunities or financial rewards, nor did I hear him talk of sacrifice and suffering. I heard a man who loved what he did and where he was. He looked and sounded fulfilled and happy with things just as they were. And as a result, he has made a difference in the lives of hundreds of boys.

When we give in a way that is authentically ours, as Coach Hurley does, we discover that something much bigger than we are is taking care of things. We relinquish control long enough to give, thereby making room in our lives for God's gifts and unexpected miracles. Faith grows amid the seemingly impossible.

This is what Jesus taught. He gave without expecting anything in return, and yet he was happy. He trusted that he would be given everything he needed in order to live life abundantly, doing exactly what he was called to do. He knew that he had been created in love and therefore was sustained by love.

Coach Hurley also demonstrates that when we give without hesitation, we think in terms of what is possible. Solutions, resources and new possibilities have a way of presenting themselves to the mind that is focused on improving a situation. We become proactive because we know that life is meant to be good for everyone, and when we find our unique niche, the Universe responds in unimaginable ways.

What Did Jesus Do?

Service challenges us once again to look at our attitude toward receiving. Instead of teaching us to sacrifice, service teaches us how to accept gifts. That may sound like a contradiction. But when we give for the pleasure of giving, we see how others get the same pleasure from sharing. We let them give to us because we know that it brings them joy, since that is our experience too. As we learned in Chapter 6, on gratitude, God gives to us through other people.

I go back to the story of the woman anointing Jesus' weary feet with luxurious oil as a wonderful illustration of how the act of receiving from another is a gift. When she ministered to Jesus, it was her way of expressing deep love and admiration for her teacher. The disciples were appalled that Jesus would allow her to do this. They said that she was wasting oil that could have been used to raise money for the poor. They also seemed to be embarrassed by the show of deep affection for Jesus. But Jesus understood that he was doing her a service by receiving her gift. He saw how she was blessed by his acceptance of her offering.

We also need to rethink the scope of service. We may believe that our service must affect others' lives in a dramatic way in order to be meaningful. People like Mother Teresa come to mind, people who gave their entire lives to the service of others. It can be intimidating—and discouraging—to think that she's the act we have to follow.

Again, Jesus demonstrated that service can come in all shapes and sizes. It can be as simple as having a conversation with someone in need, as Jesus did in his discussion with the Samaritan woman by the well. One of my favorite service stories involves the time Jesus turned water into wine during the wedding in Cana. It was his first reported miracle.

The story goes that the bride and groom had run out of wine midway through their party. This was the worst thing that could happen during a Jewish celebration, because not taking care of guests was considered to be inhospitable. Needless to say, the steward was in a panic. Mary, Jesus' mother, apprised her son of the situation. Jesus, after a bit of resistance, took his cue and changed the water into wine.

I love this miracle because of what it represents. He didn't feed a group of starving people or bring about world peace. His first miracle was to keep an ordinary couple's celebration going. It was a simple act of service that cultivated joy, with no apparent lasting impact on our world, and yet we continue to read about it centuries later. In that moment, he loved God's beloved by making sure they could continue to have a good time.

We also have a tendency to judge some acts as worthy service and others as less honorable. In truth, all service is notable. We all have the ability to contribute to the well-being of our planet, and no job is holier than another. I was reminded of this recently when I saw a vulture picking at a squirrel that had been hit and left on the side of the road. Now this is not a pretty picture, and we don't often think of vultures as doing us a service, but imagine a world where there were no scavengers. Their job is to act as the cleanup crew for Mother Earth.

However insignificant we may feel our own contribution is, we should always remember that our good works are vital to the well-being of the whole. Without our efforts, someone would suffer.

⚭

How Do You Define Service?

So far we have talked about service in terms of doing something. And our acts of service are powerful and necessary if we are going to follow in Jesus' footsteps. Yet his example calls us to go deeper, to a state of being. Jesus modeled how simply his presence served. For example, most of the time all he had to do was say a word for a miracle to occur. His powerful presence and dedication to truth were enough to assist so many others in realizing their own health and wholeness.

The Bible tells of a centurion whose servant lay in bed, paralyzed and in excruciating pain. Knowing Jesus' power, he tracked Jesus down and asked him to heal his servant. Jesus told the soldier that he would immediately come to the servant's bedside, but the centurion knew that Jesus' presence was not necessary.

He stated that Jesus simply had to say the word and his servant would be healed. He recognized that Jesus had discovered a powerful truth about the nature of illness—or rather about the illusion of sickness. He understood that Jesus' evolved presence on the planet was enough to activate the healing process.

Jesus, astounded, told him that it was already done. Because of the man's faith, Jesus didn't have to do anything but affirm what the officer already knew. But the centurion's faith grew because of the work that Jesus was doing. Jesus had evolved to the state of consciousness where he knew no illness, and he served others by helping them see it too.

We can emulate this level of wholeness. We do it by knowing who we are as divine expressions of Spirit, and our spiritual practice is the means by which we develop our spiritual awareness. Each time we sit down to meditate or study or practice one of the disciplines outlined in this book, we serve all of humanity. As we grow spiritually, we discover greater truths not only for ourselves but for everyone else. The path then becomes a bit easier for those coming after us just as Jesus made it easier for us.

And we also become nicer people to be around. Think of the people you know who have a way of making everyone around them feel comfortable and content. When we tend to our own spiritual growth, we help create a world that is kinder and gentler for everyone.

Serving others does not have to be difficult; in fact, when we are spiritually fit, it is rather easy. During morning meditation, we simply state our intention to be of service to the people we are with. Then, as we go about our day, we silently ask the questions, *How may I serve? What Truth principle wants to express through me at this moment? How can I love God's beloved?* Then we let it go. We don't define it or control it. We simply make ourselves available to Spirit.

This means looking past any false appearance to the essence of each person before us. We serve the highest ideal by seeing people as God's beloved. Imagine how differently we would treat other people if we saw them that way. We would not necessarily do anything special, yet we would treat every encounter as a sacred moment. We would breathe in each person's divine essence and communicate this to him or her through our words and presence.

We serve others by honoring them for who they really are because we open the door to possibilities they may never have thought of. Ultimately, we serve them by expecting the best for them.

Another way we serve is by being our authentic selves. When we remember who we are as blessed sons and daughters of God and act accordingly, we serve as an inspiration to others. But it is not just our good deeds that encourage others; we also serve by sharing our challenges and failures.

Life Journeys

We often hide the difficult events in our lives. We keep our pain to ourselves, thinking that no one else wants to hear it or everyone else deals with challenges more gracefully than we do. We may feel that we are being weak and ineffective when we share our difficulties. We may be afraid of being judged or rejected. But as we dig deeper into this spiritual practice, we discover that when we share our problems openly and honestly, we give others a priceless gift.

A few years ago, my younger brother was diagnosed with brain cancer. As a result of my own pain, fear and confusion,

I reached out more than I have in a very long time to old and new friends. Consequently, people called to check on me and sent cards and their good wishes. Later on, after the immediate crisis passed, they shared how they had felt useful and valued because they could give to me. I had given other people a gift when I gave them the opportunity to serve me in my hurt and anxiety.

My vulnerability gave other people permission to share their pain as well. People can quit pretending that everything is okay when they see that others have similar experiences. Life is just painful at times, and we are faced with situations that we don't know how to handle. We wonder if we are responding "correctly."

When other people are willing to share their pain, they let us know that we are not alone. We don't have to crawl off somewhere and nurse our grief until it goes away. In fact, it won't go away until we deal with it, and people help one another do that by sharing and being present.

We also serve by sharing our mistakes. We create room for others to lay down unreasonable expectations of themselves and embrace their humanity. Writer and inspirational coach Laurie Beth Jones, in her book *Jesus, CEO*, shared the story of a real estate developer who asked a team he was assembling to reveal their greatest failures. He wanted them to share what they had learned from the experience, and how the failure had made them better professionals and people.

In doing this, he fostered an environment of trust and vulnerability.[3] When we admit our mistakes, we say that it is okay not to be perfect; in fact, mistakes are expected. If we are not making mistakes, then we are living too small. When we share our imperfections, we learn to see one another more fully. We learn to love and appreciate who we are in totality.

The benefits from service are many even though they are not the reasons we do it. Sharing ourselves has been shown to be a powerful antidote for illness, depression and other ailments. People who give of themselves and contribute to the well-being of others live happier, healthier lives.

In mid-2009, Steve Hartman, the reporter for "Assignment America" on *CBS Evening News,* reported on a man named Andy Mackie who suffered from heart disease. As a result, he had undergone nine surgeries and was taking 15 medications just to stay alive. The drugs were causing such severe side effects that one day Mackie decided to stop taking them. He took the money that he would have spent on them and decided to do what he always wanted to do. He bought 300 harmonicas and gave them to children at local schools, along with free lessons.

As it turned out, he didn't die that month, so he did the same thing the next month. Month after month he took the medicine money and bought harmonicas instead. Eleven years later he is still here with us, sharing his music with anyone who wants it. At the time of the report, he had given out more than 13,000 harmonicas.

The children who were interviewed talked about how everyone loved Mackie and how, because of him, they had grown to love music. Mackie is convinced that he is alive today because he started giving back to his community. Every day, as he shares his passion with others, he feels fully alive and rich beyond measure. As a result of his incredible service, not only does the music live on, but so does Mackie.[4]

Service encompasses all this and more. When we give freely of ourselves and our abundance, we affirm God's presence in our lives. Consequently, God's love grows in us and we become the catalyst for spiritual evolution in our world. As we discover our unique gifts and develop them in a way that contributes to the well-being of others, we begin to see how we are repeating what Jesus did. We may not walk on water, but we can do things like bring music to young children and help boys go to college who had no hope of doing so. This is what it means to repeat what Jesus did. As we serve simply and purely, we add a little bit each day to Jesus' vision of a more compassionate world.

Practicing the Practice

1. Begin by asking on a daily basis, *How can I serve?* Begin to look at the people in your life as God's beloved and ask how you can love God's beloved. See yourself as the hands of God in the situation.

2. Look specifically at your gifts to determine how you can use them to assist and support others. This process goes

back to humility, and the realization that you have gifts that can benefit others. What are your gifts? Review the list you created in Chapter 7 and start looking for ways to share those gifts.

3. Start small. You don't have to jump in and dedicate many hours a week to your service. Start by looking around to see whom you can assist today with a simple task. Understand that through your actions, you are letting someone know that he or she is important.

4. Thank those people who have given to you even if it was just a simple word or gesture. We do people an incredible service when we let them know what lasting effect they have had on our lives. When we acknowledge this impact, it also makes us more aware of how we influence others. When we acknowledge others' gifts, we acknowledge our interconnectedness.

5. Begin to notice the least within your community. See those whom you would normally turn away from. Jesus told us that when we feed the hungry, we feed God. Even if you are not led to offer help physically, acknowledge their humanity. Send them a silent blessing affirming that they are cherished and part of our community too.

6. Make a better world the focus of your prayer and meditation time. Send blessings to everyone on the planet, and see a world where all God's children are happy and healthy. Then let your actions during the day match that vision.

-11-

Final Words

So where do we go from here? It may be the end of this book, but it is just the beginning of our journey. As we develop a daily routine that includes the spiritual practices that Jesus taught, we discover that we do have the power to repeat what he did; we have the same capability that Jesus possessed. It is waiting there within each of us to be developed.

Jesus showed us our unlimited capacity for love, wisdom, strength, creativity and wholeness. He opened the door to our hearts so that we might know God as intimately as he did when he was with us in person. He described heaven in glowing terms and said that we were all included. He showed us the path to follow in order to replicate his example and promised that he would be with us every step of the way. It is up to us now to accept the invitation and begin the journey.

Small Steps, Big Rewards

As I acknowledged in Chapter 1, the idea of repeating and surpassing what Jesus did can be intimidating and overwhelming to say the least. But as we incorporate spiritual practices into our lives, we discover that the greatest way to honor Jesus is to accept his invitation. We act on his faith in us.

It is like being asked to run a marathon. Most of us cannot even imagine taking on such an endeavor. But the reality is, if we did decide to run 26.2 miles, we would not start there. We would not immediately purchase a ticket to the next event and begin running without the proper equipment and training. Instead, we would start by taking walks around the block or working out in the gym. We would find others to train with and push ourselves a little farther each time.

This is no different. Like the popular slogan advised, we just do it. We begin to practice even if the voice in our head is telling us that our efforts are futile and we are sacrilegious or foolish to think we could ever be like Jesus. We trust that the simple actions we take toward the goal of emulating and surpassing Jesus will be enough to effect a change. We might even say, "Bring the body, and the mind and spirit will follow."

I happened to catch one of the final episodes of a season of *The Biggest Loser.* The premise of this reality-TV show is to follow a number of obese people who are trying to lose weight and adopt a healthier lifestyle. The contestants are taught how to eat nutritiously and participate in an intense daily exercise regimen to reshape their bodies. From what I could gather, each week the person who had lost the least amount of weight during the previous time period had to leave the show. There were four contestants left on the program I watched. That night they received their final challenge, which was to complete a full marathon.

The program showed how they continued their training to prepare themselves for the marathon. Now they had been training all along in a place called the Ranch, but when the contestants had started the process, they had no idea that they would be asked to take on this kind of undertaking at the end of the season. But you could see how, over time, each exercise had prepared them for this ultimate challenge. With each weight lifted and mile run, they were conditioning themselves for what they had once thought was impossible. And they continued their training even more intensely once they received news of the final test.

On the day of the run, each of the contestants checked in and began the 26.2-mile trek toward the finish line. They had all come to the challenge believing that there was no way they could accomplish such a huge feat. Yet individually they put one foot in front of the other, and all four of them broke the tape at the end of the race. It took one gentleman more than 13 hours to cross the finish line, but he did it.

All this seemed even more remarkable after I saw the videos the contestants had made at the start of their journeys to become fit. Each of them had talked about their frustrations and dreams. Viewers saw how they were all dangerously overweight and had difficulty even walking a short distance. Yet every step, every small change, helped them develop their ability to finish that race.

The process works the same way in the spiritual realm. When we start our sacred journey, we may be miles from our goal of emulating Jesus. However, with every prayer, act of forgiveness or expression of gratitude, we change. Our spiritual muscles grow, until one day we realize that we do have what it takes to respond to a difficult situation in a way that would make Jesus proud. We find ourselves responding with confidence and grace and in a way that serves all. We begin to see that goals that were once completely beyond our reach become not only possible but probable.

Perfection Is Not the Goal

And we don't have to do it flawlessly. The image of Jesus as the perfect holy man may overshadow our meager attempts, and we think they won't count. Because we have disconnected Jesus from his humanity, we view our own as a liability.

I go back to Coach Hurley at St. Anthony's. At one point the interviewer asked him if he was a saint. He started laughing and said something to the effect that he didn't think they allowed saints who yelled as much as he did. To punctuate his statement, there appeared a video of Hurley at a practice with his team. You could see him screaming at the kids, with an occasional cuss word bleeped out. He certainly was not presenting a picture of sainthood. Yet here he was, responsible for getting hundreds of young boys into college.[1]

When we see such an example, it challenges us to confront our assumptions about what goodness looks or sounds like. Keep in mind that the Bible tells stories in a dramatic fashion. The writers took liberties, sharing only the highlights and embellishing those to make their point. We don't read about the times Jesus failed. There are a few stories of Jesus becoming angry and frustrated, but most of the time he is portrayed as a calm, peaceful man. My hunch is that there were many times during his evolution when he did not have the faith, strength, patience or wisdom to succeed in what he was attempting to do. He, too, had to develop his awareness of Spirit so that God could work through him.

And you don't have to bite off the whole chunk. You can make the process easier by picking one practice instead of doing all nine at once. Each practice is a dynamo in itself. By concentrating on a single practice, you will automatically effect change in yourself and others.

You will also see how the practices are intertwined. Just try praying the way Jesus taught without also practicing humility, faith, vision, forgiveness and gratitude. They are all part of the prayer process. Similarly, the practice of forgiveness leads to gratitude and community. And service is the foundation of all of them.

Once you've chosen a practice, decide on a few of the activities at the end of the chapter to implement each day. Pay attention to how your chosen practice is related to the others. Notice how you automatically begin to include others. You may find yourself concentrating on one practice for a while and then moving on to another.

Note the changes in yourself and observe how you are also making a difference in the lives of those around you. Sometimes you can see the impact right away, and sometimes it takes a while. Remember, this is a lifelong process.

No Instant Gratification

We also need to develop patience. Our fast-food society creates the illusion that everything should happen instantaneously, and if it doesn't, then we must be doing something wrong. The conversation in our heads often goes something like this: *I prayed this morning and nothing happened. So let me pray for the week. Still nothing is happening, so I must not be doing it right, or this must not work.*

In order to be effective, we must understand that our evolution is not a quick process. At a time when we can witness events across the globe the instant they happen, day or night, the spiritual life challenges us to persevere. To take this concept even further, we must ask whether or not we are willing to start something that may not mature in our lifetime. Are we willing to run a relay race, handing off the baton of our contribution, knowing that we may never see the final victory?

It becomes even more important to celebrate the small victories as we go. If we can relax and see that we are undertaking a lifetime commitment, we take so much of the pressure off ourselves. We accept that when we sign on to evolve to the level of Jesus, we give up the idea that there is a place to arrive and instead see life as a continuous process of growth and possibility.

If we judge what Jesus envisioned and what he actually accomplished by contemporary standards, he would be considered a colossal failure. There were still wars. People were still being persecuted and going hungry. People continued to misunderstand God and their relationship to Spirit. They were afraid, lonely, hurting and sick. Jesus stayed the course in the face of what appeared to be insurmountable odds.

He took powerful principles that were available to everyone and gave them new meaning. He was able to bring spiritual teachings alive in a way that reverberates today. Jesus knew that he was simply planting the seeds and it would take time for them to take root and grow. Along the way, his message has been ignored and perverted, used to kill and condemn. If he were still in the tomb, he would be rolling over in it.

Jesus understood how difficult his message was. He knew as he was teaching that the people listening were barely getting what he was talking about. As told in a story in Matthew,

Jesus was asleep in a boat with the disciples after an especially dramatic display of God's power. He had just finished feeding 5,000 people by multiplying the fish and the loaves, manifesting so much food that there were 12 baskets left over. Jesus and the disciples had jumped in the boat and headed out to the Sea of Galilee to escape the throngs of fans.

So there they are in the boat when Jesus' disciples realized that someone had forgotten to bring dinner. As we all might have done, they started arguing about it. You can just hear their voices: "Hey, who was supposed to bring the bread and fish? I don't see it anywhere."

"Not me, that's Peter's job."

"I thought you were bringing it. Why is it always up to me to take care of everything?"

"Who is going to tell Jesus that you messed up?"

Jesus then woke up and admonished them. He said in Matthew 16:8-10: "You of little faith, why are you talking about having no bread? Do you still not perceive? Do you not remember the five loaves for the five thousand, and how many baskets you gathered?" Can you imagine his frustration? We forget so easily that God is always present and active.

Yet he continued, even when faced with such a lack of understanding by those closest to him. He continued his mission because he was convinced that eventually, people would comprehend what he was teaching and would begin to incorporate his lessons into their lives.

How to Surpass Jesus, Practice by Practice

Now is the time for those teachings to take on a whole new meaning. We are in a stage of unprecedented growth of soul and spirit, and as a species we are making huge evolutionary leaps in single generations. More and more we understand how our actions affect the whole. Quantum physics has shown that we do nothing in isolation; rather, every thought, word and deed affects our world in some way. More and more people are realizing a desire to make a difference.

Until now, I have kept the discussion focused mainly on how we can achieve the same level as Jesus. But what about surpassing him? He said that those of us who believe in him would do what he did, and even greater things. But how can we make that happen? First we must be able to see ourselves as Jesus' equals waiting to be realized. As each of us claims our spiritual potential and joins with others around the world, we will learn that we can repeat what he did, and as we do, our world will change accordingly. This is what it will take to surpass what Jesus did.

One look around, and we can see a plethora of evidence to support this observation. A spiritual evolution is sweeping the planet. People are hungry for spiritual substance that has depth and staying power. Oprah Winfrey and author Eckhart Tolle reached millions with their webcast series studying the book *A New Earth* by Tolle. As more and more people connect with the intention of growing spiritually, we will gather a force that propels humankind into realms undiscovered by Jesus or any other spiritual master. Our collective effort will bring about radical, unimaginable change—and the kingdom of God here on earth.

Let's review the practices and examine their collective impact.

• First there is the practice of **visioning**. It is the deliberate act of seeing what is possible and forming your life around that dream. Jesus knew what was possible and kept it at the forefront of everything he did. As an individual man in a small, obscure corner of the world 2,000 years ago, without any of the resources at his disposal that we have today, he was able to change the very nature of humankind itself. He had a vision of a world in which every man, woman and child would know how precious he or she was in the eyes of God.

Imagine what would be possible if this vision took hold of the masses. What if an entire group of people dedicated themselves to the dream of a fulfilled, happy life for everyone? With clarity and purpose, our collective decisions and actions would become aligned to make this dream a reality.

• The second practice is **faith**. As we join with others, we come to know God in many forms and names. Yet underneath the diverse experiences of God is the common thread of all that is holy. Our world has seen an explosion of religions transcending cultures and other boundaries, and people all over the globe are incorporating different aspects of other faith traditions into their own practice. Devout Christians are meditating, and the Dalai Lama quotes Jesus. Appreciation and understanding grow with every exchange.

• Then we **pray**. As we change, our prayers change, and our prayers gather power as we pray collectively. We know that prayer can change our personal lives, and when we join with others, prayer becomes a powerful agent of change worldwide. Deepak Chopra, in his book *Peace Is the Way*, cited the work that James Twyman has done with prayer as the way to peace. Twyman organizes prayer vigils in hot spots around the world and gets immediate results. Chopra gave the example of a vigil that Twyman led on February 9, 2004, in Jerusalem, connecting with people all over the world via the Internet. According to Chopra, statistics showed that the following day, violence in the West Bank fell by 50 percent or more.[2]

• Next is **forgiveness**, which develops our capacity for deep compassion and concern for others. Imagine if an entire nation dedicated itself to the practice of forgiveness. Wars would cease. Attack and the need for revenge would become obsolete. No longer would there be us and them; we would become one. This is what Jesus envisioned, and when we join others in this practice, it becomes possible.

In *Peace Is the Way*, Chopra offered a seven-day prescription for peace that we can practice on our own. He asserted that as we grow in peaceful consciousness, we will cultivate peace on our planet. Forgiveness aids this process because it is impossible to harbor anger and resentment and be at peace at the same time.[3]

• **Gratitude**, it has been said, is stronger than love. We have talked about the power of gratitude in our own lives; now imagine if an entire group of people were dedicated simply to feeling grateful. There would be no room for hatred or jealousy or anger or criticism. Everyone's function would be to feel and express appreciation for those around them.

When people feel appreciated, they start to believe in themselves. There is nothing stopping them from taking risks. People recognize the essence of who they are and act accordingly because they see themselves reflected in the eyes of others.

As we practice gratitude together, we recognize and give thanks for our abundance. We become compelled to share our prosperity in life-affirming ways and feel personally responsible for ensuring that every person has the resources necessary to live a rich, wholesome life.

• In practicing **humility**, we recognize and share our gifts freely and fearlessly, ensuring a just and sustainable world for everyone. Humility practiced collectively fosters a sense of the sacred in each of us. We bow before the face of God with every interaction. We recognize the gifts in others while offering them the love and support they need to cultivate their talents. They, in turn, experience the joy that comes from sharing their genius with others.

• Then we share what we have learned in our **community**. Our community today is no longer just our neighborhood, city or country; it is our world. Chopra talked about the way peace will be obtained when we no longer see ourselves in terms of nationalities but as spiritual beings responsible for the well-being of the entire planet. We are no longer American, French or Chinese. We are world citizens.

• We learn to let go and fully live when we practice **death**. The spiritual practice of death calls us to stay present for the endings and the good-byes, encouraging us to feel the depth of the loss so that we may make room for the new life waiting to emerge. Jesus showed us that on the other side of every death—be it physical, emotional or spiritual—is a new beginning. When we embrace death as a practice, we come to trust the process of death and resurrection.

• Then, finally, **service**. Think of the changes that would result if each of us adopted an attitude of joyful service. If my task were to serve your well-being, the very nature of life would become unrecognizable. My own life would be rich beyond measure because I would be living it the way it should be lived.

This may sound like a pipe dream, but it is what Jesus saw and charged us with when he told us to do greater things. We start by repeating what he did, and as we do that together, we will find that we are surpassing what he did in ways that not even he could have imagined. But we must start.

When I was a teacher, one of the school administrators would tell the same story at the beginning of every school year as we were getting ready for students: A young man was walking along a beach riddled with starfish that were dumped on shore at high tide. Unless they returned to the water soon, they would all die.

As he walked down the beach, he picked up starfish one at a time and threw them back into the ocean. Along came another man watching him, confused by his actions. He went up to the young man and asked him what he was doing. The young man answered that he was "saving starfish."

The observer then asked how he could think he was making a difference, when there were so many starfish littering the beach. The young man silently picked up one more starfish and flung it far out into the sea, turned to the older gentleman and said, "I made a difference for that one."

That is what our endeavors will seem like more often than not. We will wonder if we are doing something right, if we are doing any good, if we are getting anywhere close to what Jesus exemplified and taught. But then we will be able to look down the beach of our lives and see that our actions made a difference in the lives of others—and in our own.

Jesus understood that the finished product is not the important piece. What we do on a daily basis is what matters most. When we follow in his footsteps, we commit to the practice for the sake of the practice. It commands deep faith and surrender as we let go of agendas, results, outcomes and recognition. We do it because we are compelled by his vision, his presence, his promise. We, too, long to experience the Divine as he did, to be able to serve our world deeply.

So I reissue my invitation. I ask you to join me on this journey of growth and evolution. I ask you to join me as I take my own first fragile steps along the path that Jesus laid out for us. Come with me, and together we can continue the work that he started. Come with me, and together we can do greater things.

Practicing the Practice

1. First of all, congratulations for completing the journey. You made it! As I said at the beginning of the book, you are free to pick up any old beliefs that still serve you.

2. I encourage you to write about your overall impressions of what you have learned. How has your perspective of Jesus changed? Can you imagine repeating what he did in some small way?

3. Have you started a practice? If so, good for you. If not, pick one of the nine, and for a week, incorporate it into your daily routine. Journal about the results.

4. Find a community to join forces with. There are myriad online groups, New Thought churches and study groups that pursue this line of thinking. Join them to increase your

power and effectiveness. Please feel free to contact me at *www.unitychurchoflife.com* for support and to let me know how you are doing.

5. Remember to breathe as you go forward, and feel the love and support of Spirit all around you. Feel my love around you as together we set out to repeat individually and surpass collectively what Jesus modeled.

Endnotes

Chapter 1

[1] Cynthia Bourgeault. *Encountering the Wisdom Jesus: Quickening the Kingdom of Heaven Within.* (Audio CD), Boulder, CO: Sounds True, Inc., 2005.

[2] Marcus J. Borg. *Meeting Jesus Again for the First Time: The Historical Jesus and the Heart of Contemporary Faith.* San Francisco: Harper, 1995.

Chapter 2

[1] Marcus J. Borg, *Meeting Jesus Again for the First Time: The Historical Jesus and the Heart of Contemporary Faith.*

[2] Ibid.

[3] Thomas Moore. *Care of the Soul: A Guide for Cultivating Depth and Sacredness in Everyday Life.* New York: Harper Paperbacks, 1992.

Chapter 3

[1] Michael Dowd. *Thank God for Evolution: How the Marriage of Science and Religion Will Transform Your Life and Our World.* San Francisco: Council Oaks Books, 2007.

2 Ibid.

3 Eric Butterworth. *Spiritual Economics: The Principles and Process of True Prosperity.* Unity Village, MO: Unity House, 1998.

4 Ibid.

5 Greg Mortenson. *Three Cups of Tea: One Man's Mission to Promote Peace . . . One School at a Time.* New York: Penguin, 2007.

6 Myrtle Fillmore. *Healing Letters.* Unity Village, MO: Unity House, 1954.

Chapter 4

1 Thomas Keating. *Open Mind, Open Heart: The Contemplative Dimension of the Gospel.* New York: Continuum, 2000.

2 Wayne Muller. *Learning to Pray: How We Find Heaven on Earth.* New York: Bantam, 2003.

3 Myrtle Fillmore, *Healing Letters.*

4 "A Conversation About the Future of Medicine." Perspectives on medicine and healthcare. N.p., n.d. Web. 27 Oct. 2009 <www.dosseydossey.com/larry/default.html>

5 Gregg Braden. *Secrets of the Lost Mode of Prayer: The Hidden Power of Beauty, Blessings, Wisdom, and Hurt.* Carlsbad, CA: Hay House, 2006.

6 Charles Fillmore, *The Revealing Word,* Unity Village, MO: Unity House, 1959.

7 Wayne Muller, *Learning to Pray: How We Find Heaven on Earth.*

Chapter 5

1 "All Is Forgiven?" *CBS Sunday Morning*. CBS. n.p., 12 Apr. 2009. Web. 14 Apr. 2009 <http://www.cbsnews.com/stories/2009/04/12/sunday/main4937311.shtml>

2 Bruce Lipton. *The Biology of Belief: Unleashing the Power of Consciousness, Matter & Miracles*. Carlsbad, CA: Hay House, 2008.

3 "All Is Forgiven?" *CBS Sunday Morning*.

4 "Fatal Shooting at U.S. Amish School." *BBC News*. BBC News, Oct. 2006. Web. 22 Jan. 2007. <http://news.bbc.co.uk/2/hi/5400570.stm>

5 Gary Simmons. *The I of the Storm: Embracing Conflict, Creating Peace*, Unity Village, MO: Unity House, 2001.

6 Dr. Helen Schucman. (Foundation for Inner Peace), *A Course in Miracles: Combined Volume*. New York: Viking, 1996.

7 Louise L. Hay. *You Can Heal Your Life*. Carlsbad, CA: Hay House, 1984.

8 Gary Simmons, *The I of the Storm*.

Chapter 6

1 Charles Fillmore. *Prosperity*. Unity Village, MO: Unity House, 1936.

2 Gregg Braden. *The Isaiah Effect: Decoding the Lost Science of Prayer and Prophecy*. New York: Three Rivers Press, 2000.

3 Ibid.

4 Ibid.

5 Ibid.

Do Greater Things

6 Eric Butterworth, *Spiritual Economics: The Principles and Process of True Prosperity.*

7 "An Uphill Battle." *CBS Sunday Morning.* CBS. n.p., 21 Oct. 2007. Web. 26 Oct. 2007 <http://www.cbsnews.com/stories/2007/10/21/sunday/main3389200.shtml> Story retold with permission from subject Ralph Green.

8 Jacqueline Bascobert Kelm. *Appreciative Living: The Principles of Appreciative Inquiry in Personal Life.* Wake Forest, NC: Venet, 2005.

9 Jacqueline Bascobert Kelm. *The Joy of Appreciative Living: Your 28-Day Plan to Greater Happiness in 3 Incredibly Easy Steps.* New York: Tarcher/Penguin, 2008.

Chapter 7

1 Walter Wink. *The Powers That Be: Theology for a New Millennium.* New York: Galilee/Doubleday, 1998.

2 Wayne Muller. *How, Then, Shall We Live? Four Simple Questions That Reveal the Beauty and Meaning of Our Lives.* New York: Bantam, 1997.

Chapter 8

1 Marshall B. Rosenberg, Ph.D. *Nonviolent Communication: A Language of Life.* Encinitas, CA: Puddledancer Press, 2003.

2 Michael Dowd, *Thank God for Evolution: How the Marriage of Science and Religion Will Transform Your Life and Our World.*

[3] Barbara Marx Hubbard. *Humanity Ascending Series, Part 1: Our Story* (DVD). Quantum Production, 2006.

Chapter 9

[1] John Shelby Spong. *Jesus for the Non-Religious*. New York: HarperOne, 2007.

[2] Marcus J. Borg. *The Heart of Christianity: Rediscovering a Life of Faith*. New York: HarperOne, 2003.

[3] "The Guru and the Pandit: A Vow to Live Forever." Andrew Cohen and Ken Wilber. *What Is Enlightenment?* Issue 30, Sept.-Nov. 2005. <www.enlightennext.org/magazine/j30/gurupandit.asp>

Chapter 10

[1] Marcus J. Borg, *The Heart of Christianity: Rediscovering a Life of Faith*.

[2] "Holding Court and Performing Miracles." *CBS Sunday Morning*. CBS. n.p., 5 May 2009. Web. 9 May 2009. <http://www.cbsnews.com/stories/2009/04/03/sunday/main4917067.shtml> Story retold with permission from subject Bob Hurley.

[3] Laurie Beth Jones. *Jesus, CEO: Using Ancient Wisdom for Visionary Leadership*. New York: Hyperion, 1996.

4 "Modern Pied Piper Cheats Death." *CBS Evening News*. CBS. n.p., 3 May 2009. Web. 9 May 2009. <http://www.cbsnews.com/stories/2009/05/01/assignment_america/main4984493.shtml> Story retold with permission from subject Andy Mackie.

Chapter 11

1 "Holding Court and Performing Miracles," *CBS Sunday Morning*.

2 Deepak Chopra. *Peace Is the Way: Bringing War and Violence to an End*. New York: Three Rivers Press, 2005.

3 Ibid.

Acknowledgements

This book bears my name but there are so many hands that have their fingerprints on it. If I tried to list everyone, I know I would have to leave someone out because the list would be so long. With that said, I want to give special thanks to the following people:

To Rev. Marjorie Kass, my first Unity minister who patiently loved me as I struggled to believe that these principles weren't too good to be true. For Rev. Richard Rogers, my minister in Phoenix who said it didn't matter what I called Jesus as long as I opened my heart to him.

To Charlotte Rains Dixon, who patiently and lovingly provided me feedback during my entire writing process. You had such wonderful things to say even after the 10th reading.

To Unity House for taking a chance on me and providing me love and support every step of the way to bring this book into physical reality.

To my wonderful spiritual community, where it has been my humbled honor to serve the past 10 years. You all have loved me and believed in me in a way that made success a certainty.

To my mother, who gave me an old Underwood typewriter because she recognized the writer in me. You have always heard my dreams and kept them close to your heart as if they were your own.

To my husband Michael, for his constant presence and love for the past 23 years. I know I would not be the person I am today without you in my life.

To the "gang" for constantly whispering your love and guidance into my ears and heart.

And finally, to Jesus for his willingness to blaze the trail so we could follow in his footsteps to finally create a world where the Kingdom of Heaven is the norm.

About the Author

Rev. Felicia Blanco Searcy is founding minister of Unity Church of Life in Murfreesboro, Tennessee. She has published numerous articles and is also a contributing writer to *Sacred Secrets: Finding Your Way to Joy, Peace and Prosperity* (Unity House). She is a regular guest on Unity.FM's *Hooked on Classics* (*www.unity.fm*). Before becoming a minister, Felicia worked as a speech therapist, third grade teacher and adjunct instructor of education at Middle Tennessee State University. She has been a Truth student since 1986 and is dedicated to bringing the transformative Unity teachings to all corners of the world. She lives in Murfreesboro with her husband Michael, her two dogs and her cat.

B0087